UNPROFITABLE RELATIONSHIP: Healing the broken hearted

... 50 Questions and Answers

BY

BOLA ADEWARA

First Edition 2020

Published by:

E-life Books

Aladelola Street, Ikosi Ketu, Lagos, Nigeria.

Tel: +234 8057849480, 2348092343463

E-mail: bola@bolaadewara.com

Website: www.bolaadewara.com

TABLE OF CONTENT

ENDORSEMENTS....6

DEDICATION....15

INTRODUCTION....16

UNPROFITABLE RELATIONSHIP 1:....18

UNPROFITABLE RELATIONSHIP 2:....27

UNPROFITABLE RELATIONSHIP 3:....33

UNPROFITABLE RELATIONSHIP 4:....38

UNPROFITABLE RELATIONSHIP 5:....44

UNPROFITABLE RELATIONSHIP 6:....52

UNPROFITABLE RELATIONSHIP 7:....57

UNPROFITABLE RELATIONSHIP 8:....64

UNPROFITABLE RELATIONSHIP 9:....71

UNPROFITABLE RELATIONSHIP 10:....79

UNPROFITABLE RELATIONSHIP 11:....83

UNPROFITABLE RELATIONSHIP 12:....88

UNPROFITABLE RELATIONSHIP 13:....96

UNPROFITABLE RELATIONSHIP 14:....103

UNPROFITABLE RELATIONSHIP 15:....107

UNPROFITABLE RELATIONSHIP 16:....112

UNPROFITABLE RELATIONSHIP 17: 119
UNPROFITABLE RELATIONSHIP 18: 122
UNPROFITABLE RELATIONSHIP: 19....129
UNPROFITABLE RELATIONSHIP: 20....134
UNPROFITABLE RELATIONSHIP: 21....139
UNPROFITABLE RELATIONSHIP: 22....150
UNPROFITABLE RELATIONSHIP: 23....156
UNPROFITABLE RELATIONSHIP: 24....162
UNPROFITABLE RELATIONSHIP: 25....167
UNPROFITABLE RELATIONSHIP: 26....172
UNPROFITABLE RELATIONSHIP: 27....177
UNPROFITABLE RELATIONSHIP: 28....182
UNPROFITABLE RELATIONSHIP: 29....186
UNPROFITABLE RELATIONSHIP: 30....191
UNPROFITABLE RELATIONSHIP: 31....196
UNPROFITABLE RELATIONSHIP: 32....200
UNPROFITABLE RELATIONSHIP: 33....208
UNPROFITABLE RELATIONSHIP: 34....213
UNPROFITABLE RELATIONSHIP: 35....222
UNPROFITABLE RELATIONSHIP: 36....229

UNPROFITABLE RELATIONSHIP: 37 238

UNPROFITABLE RELATIONSHIP: 38 242

UNPROFITABLE RELATIONSHIP: 39 252

UNPROFITABLE RELATIONSHIP: 40 255

UNPROFITABLE RELATIONSHIP: 41 259

UNPROFITABLE RELATIONSHIP: 42 265

UNPROFITABLE RELATIONSHIP: 43 269

UNPROFITABLE RELATIONSHIP: 44 274

UNPROFITABLE RELATIONSHIP: 45 278

UNPROFITABLE RELATIONSHIP: 46 286

UNPROFITABLE RELATIONSHIP: 47 290

UNPROFITABLE RELATIONSHIP: 48 295

UNPROFITABLE RELATIONSHIP: 49 300

UNPROFITABLE RELATIONSHIP: 50 304

ABOUT THE BOOK 308

ABOUT THE AUTHOR 310

BOOKS FROM THE SAME AUTHOR 311

ENDORSEMENTS

THIS BOOK IS AN EXCELLENT PACKAGE OF SUCH COUNSEL

Though many marriages are troubled today, the situation is not a black market where people buy items they cannot examine before purchasing. However, the buyer will have to accept and use the already bought item the way it is. There is always a way out of every troubled marriage if the individual or couple concerned seeks God who does great and marvellous things, including resolving conflicts in marriages. No one can see God physically, but we can see Him through wise, godly counsels His servants give. That is precisely what this book is about. These divine counsels are like rain to the thirsty land, which comforts those mourning. At this moment, I recommend the book to as many as can lay their hands on it. You do not need to grope in the dark anymore if you have challenges in your marriage. There is safety in godly counsels. This book is an excellent package of such counsels. It is a guide for now and a compass for the future. It is a Blessing!

Rev Janet Onaolapo,

Genera Overseer, Abundant Life Gospel Church, Lagos, Nigeria.

IT IS BETTER TO LEARN FROM OTHERS' EXAMPLES THAN FROM PERSONAL EXPERIENCES

Going through the manuscript was thoroughly exhilarating. I can confidently call this book a masterpiece because of the significant ensemble of life stories that touch the heart and great counsels that bring healing and peace.

Some experiences are bound to occur in your life as you take steps to be joined by another person. When you read this book, you will know how to navigate your life and relationship to go through some of the experiences mentioned. After all, it is better to learn from others' examples than from personal experiences.

I, therefore, recommend this masterpiece for everyone: old couples, young couples, engaged, yet to be engaged, and even those who are not ready to enter into the marriage institution. I assure you, it is going to be a great read.

Rev. (Mrs) Oyeladun O. Ayorinde,

Abeokuta, Ogun State, Nigeria.

THE AUTHOR HAS ALSO POSTULATED THAT A MAN IS THE LEADER OF HIS HOME AND, AS SUCH, MUST LIVE BY HIGHER STANDARDS THAN HIS WIFE

The rate of divorce and separation in society today is alarming, and the flimsy reasons for the divorce are much more alarming. It has become a source of concern for Christian leaders and others who understand the mind of God for marriage. In this book, Pastor Bola Adewara has delved into the root of marital issues. He has shed light on the fact that marriage is man's ordained responsibility.

Through the wise counsels given to each issue, he has been able to, in simple terms, explain the fact that Christian marriage is a heterosexual and monogamous union. It involves the loving, lifelong commitment of each to the other and should not be entered into unadvisedly, but by a public leaving of parents and should be consummated in an exclusive sexual union. The author has also postulated that a man is the leader of his home and, as such, must live by higher standards than his wife. Leadership is a journey and not a destination. A common problem identified in the different marriages and relationships in the book is incompatibility and lack of understanding of what marriage entails. I recommend this book for everybody- married, single, those in courtship, marriage counsellors, and every other person who desires more knowledge in marriage affairs.

Rev. Mrs. Adetutu Coker,

The King's Chamber, Lagos, Nigeria.

THE BOOK IS AN INVALUABLE PRE-MARRIAGE AND

AFTER MARRIAGE RESOURCE

This book demystifies the uncertainty about what couples should expect in marriage with the real-life stories and experiences they can learn from and take necessary precautions. Although most of the stories shared are unpleasant experiences, the book offers valuable insights on possible realities couples, especially women, should brace up for and know how to handle such situations if they arise.

The stories, along with the well-articulated counsel for each case, make the book an invaluable pre-marriage and after marriage resource for both singles and the married. I fully recommend the book for all who desire a happy married life.

Lekan Otufodunrin,

Executive Director, Media Career Development Network (MCDN), Lagos, Nigeria.

AS AN AUTHOR OF MANY BOOKS ON MARRIAGE AND FAMILY LIFE, I KNOW WHEN A MARRIAGE BOOK IS GOOD. THIS IS ONE OF THEM

I understand that asking the right questions and from the right person is one of the best ways to learn. Marriage around the world is having severe issues. People have many questions, but not many people can offer answers that will help. This book by Bola Adewara is a timely effort to answer people's questions in very practical, easy-to-use, blunt, and even a times brutal yet humorous ways. Reading it looks like reading many marriage books simultaneously or visiting a counsellor or a marriage therapist. As an author of many books on marriage and family life, I know when a marriage book is good. This is one of them. I dare you to read it to the end.

Bisi Adewale,

Familybooster Ministry International, Lagos, Nigeria.

YOU CAN'T BE BORED READING THROUGH THIS COLLECTION. THE BOOK WILL MAKE YOU CRY, LAUGH AND REFLECT

Bola Adewara's **RELATIONSHIP: Healing the**

broken hearted ... *50 Questions and Answers;* is a collection of different marriage experiences. It is a mirror that showcases issues of infidelity, economic strangulation, bareness, and all sorts of marital challenges with an attendant pill of counsel for each of the issues raised. Reading through the book gives you an overview of what it looks like to have a challenged marriage. The counsel given to each experience is the utility end of the book. So, the author is not just presenting a problem, he is also offering a solution. You can't be bored reading through this collection. The book will make you cry, laugh and reflect. It is a practical guide for every married person who desires a good home. The book is not just another addition to books on marriage; rather, it is an exquisite addition that informs and empathises with the reader. ***Gbenga Osinaike,***

Publisher, Church Times, Lagos, Nigeria.

THIS BOOK IS A MUST-READ FOR THOSE

WHO SEEK WISDOM FOR MARRIAGE, RELATIONSHIPS, AND LIFE IN GENERAL

".... a practical, easy-to-read compilation of everyday marriage and relationship stories, shared from the heart, that people of different ages and marital statuses can identify with. Accentuated with sound and godly counsels and backed up with appropriate Scriptures, this book is a must-read for those who seek wisdom for marriage, relationships, and life in general."

Debola Atoyebi,

President, Interdenominational Pastors' Wives Forum (IPWF).

I ENDORSE AND RECOMMEND THIS BOOK AS A TOOL OF HEALING COUNSEL AND VITAL INFORMATION FOR COUPLES

This book is a treasure, especially with the broadness of its scope. It is not only a must-have for couples in marriage but for young people about to get into it. Marriages are under many attacks because people go into it without the proper information. I endorse and recommend this book as a tool of healing counsel and vital information for couples.

Sopeolu Ilori,

Lead Pastor, Revival Assembly TLC (The Lekki Church) Lagos Nigeria. Convener, Relationship Clinic with Pastor Sope.

DEDICATION

This book is dedicated to people who have gone through squabbles and serious disagreements in their relationships and matrimonies, especially those who have lost their lives in the course of it. If they had had access to a book like this or were properly mentored in relationships, they would probably have been wiser and averted the pains.

INTRODUCTION

When I started posting my thoughts on different issues on Social media, I never knew that it would take the turn of counselling. My idea was to write on any topic: church, politics, relationship, marriage, mentoring, youth, empowerment, government, etc. Gradually, I began to receive emails from people who were touched by my postulations. It was a rude shock to me when, one day, a lady called me and asked if she could send me emails about her matrimonial challenges. I told her to speak to her pastor or an elder in her Church rather than seek counsel from Social media. She responded that her story could end up becoming a sermon topic on a Sunday, and she would become the talk of the Church. Like so many other people after her, she was not confident that their Church leaders could keep sealed lips on members' challenges.

When I posted the first mail, many people responded to it. This encouraged the other ones on my friends' list to also send in their mails, all hiding behind the anonymity of social media to receive counsel. Compiled here are 50 cases sent to me by different people. I refused to copy the various counsels given on social media because some were very biblical but not balanced, some funny, some ridiculous, and practically untenable.

To make this book worthwhile, I sought the support of some balanced Bible teachers and preachers of the Word to offer informed, critical counsel after each case. Rev Gboyega Adejobi of Lifeline Bible Church, Agege Lagos, Nigeria, and Pastor Sina Oladimeji, a Bible teacher too, have been of great help in this regard. I subsequently ran these counsels through the biblical eyes of preachers like Dr. Mrs. Jane Onaolapo, General Overseer, Abundant Life Gospel Church, Rev. Mrs. Adetutu Coker of The King's Chamber, Rev. Mrs. Oyeladun O. Ayorinde, and Pastor Mrs. FolaBola Tijani, so that apart from being a good read, this book would be a mentoring resource for couples and the younger generation preparing for marriage.

UNPROFITABLE RELATIONSHIP 1:
HOW I FOUND JOY IN MY BARRENNESS

Rather than remain unhappy and lonely in an abusive relationship over her inability to conceive, a woman decided to adopt two children after walking out of the marriage. Here, she narrates her journey from sadness to joy and advises women in a similar condition to learn from her experience, act fast, and believe that God is not finished with them yet.

"I read one of your posts on a childless woman, and I felt I needed to speak on the pains I went through in the hands of men, especially my husband, and how God wiped my tears. I want to encourage someone with this story to know God is never finished with anybody.

Up till my final year at the university, I knew no man. That would tell you that I was not promiscuous. I was raised in a mission house, where all we knew was Church. Even in Church, no man would dare speak about love to us; we would run. When I was in the university, each time I saw my friends with their boyfriends, I saw them as sinners. It was when they were talking about getting married after graduation that it dawned on me that I had no boyfriend. Some of my friends began to warn me to be careful with my 'holy, holy' way of life. It was not that guys were not coming to me, but I rebuffed them.

The first relationship I eventually had was during my NYSC in Jos. This guy seemed like the man I could marry. I was inexperienced. I did not know how one thing led to the other, and he slept with me. The first person! What did he not promise? He would marry me. He was amazed to see a virgin at 25. He promised to take me to meet his parents, etc. I felt, at last, God had justified my chastity. I allowed him regular sex because I thought I had found my husband. I shared all I had with him; all my money and foodstuff. During my NYSC, we lived like husband and wife. How my life turned from a holy girl to a wayward girl still beats my imagination. Maybe it was due to pressure from friends. I never knew that life was so deceptive.

The last day of our service year, when we were given the discharge certificates, was the last day I saw my husband-to-be. How he sneaked out on me to his room and packed and left Jos remains a mystery to me. When I did not see him on the second day, I was nearly mad. I mean, MAD!

The biggest shock came when I got back home in Ibadan and discovered that I was pregnant; I was two months gone – daughter of a pastor? We thought it was delayed menstruation because of *jedijedi* (pile). It was in the hospital that mum was told I was two months gone. Anyway, my mum had a close friend, a nurse in the Church, who invited me to her home. I explained the whole story, how the guy ran away. She decided on her own, and the pregnancy was aborted. The first fruit of my womb! Do I need to recount the agony?

I was lucky to get a job, and the agony led me into another relationship. I felt I needed to move on after much counselling by the nurse. She encouraged me to fall in love again, and I did. In two years, I got married to a guy. That was in 1998. We lived in Abuja. He was a calm gentleman. Our home was peaceful and nice. But, somehow, I could not conceive.

After about three years, anxiety set in. Gradually the home I knew as peaceful became another thing. The man I thought was cool, calm, and collected became a jerk, a philanderer, an adulterer, an abuser of wife, and a drunk! Just under three years of childless marriage, I became depressed and worried. I began to run from pillar to post. My mum died in a motor accident along Lokoja-Abuja road over this issue on her way to see me.

The biggest shock came in 2007 when I discovered

that my husband already had three children from another woman. I never knew my husband had married another woman after three years of living with him. He could not just wait.

Medically, I was told nothing was wrong with me. Doctors said it baffles them why I could not get pregnant. I did not know where the evil or challenge came from. Later on, my husband became insane with beatings and abuses, telling me to leave his house. I was told to move out; after all, he had a wife somewhere.

I worked with a blue-chip, earned well, and was doing great. In 2007, I told my boss that I wanted to leave Abuja for any other state. My boss understood what I was going through. She approved of Lagos. But before I moved, my boss, who had a similar problem, called me to her house, where she advised me to consider adopting a child.

I was 46, and I was getting the early menopausal signs. It was a harrowing experience to accept that I would not carry my child in my womb. I agreed. And she gave me letters and stood for me as my guarantor in two places. I adopted two children; both were less than a month old, from two different locations in different towns.

I relocated to Lagos with the children. So, no one around knew my story. They all thought I had just been put to bed and everybody called me *Mama ibeji (*Mother of Twins*)*. The babies sucked my breasts, even in public. The boy and the girl have grown to know me as their mum. I have accepted them in my subconsciousness as my biological twins. I told people their father died when I was pregnant with them.

I put up two buildings, four flats each in their names. They are both in one of the best elementary schools in Lagos. We travel. They have seen the world. I have my children now. I know that these children would give me the children I could not bear. They bear my father's name.

And for you to know how God works, these children now look alike. The same complexion, same faces, same height, hairy, and people tell me they look like me. How this happened, I do not know. But it convinced me that God did it. I believe it is God's way of telling me He is with me. Those who wait upon the Lord shall renew their strength.

I do not feel I am barren anymore. Some of my old friends who thought I was barren do not know my story because none of them saw me or knew where I was for close to eight years. The two people who knew my story were my boss (late now) and the place where I adopted them from. By the way, I do not even care if anybody knows.

I have given this testimony so that people like me who thought God had finished with them on account of conception would have hope to live again. I have hope and high expectations. He turned my mourning into dancing again. He lifted my sorrows. I cannot stay silent.

COUNSEL:

Your testimony is inspiring and encouraging. It bolsters the fact that, indeed, weeping may endure for a night, but joy will still come in the morning (Psalm 30: 5). However, there is this aspect you need to resolve as soon as possible so you will not be living a lie. Someday, somewhere, sometime, somehow, you will have to tell your adopted children their true story and let them know you're not their biological mother. You will also need to make all the important people in your life see this truth. Already, you have given everybody around you the wrong impression that you are their biological mother whereas you are not but for how long do you want to continue living in such a lie? Lying is a grievous sin before God. Please, meditate on Psalm 5: 6; John 8: 32; 2Corinthians 13: 8; 1Peter 3: 10, and Revelation 21: 8. Jesus is Truth personified (John 14: 6), and the Holy Spirit

is the Spirit of Truth (John 14: 17; 15: 26; 16: 13 & 1John 4: 6).

Adoption is part of the realities of life we are yet to fully accept in this part of the world (even in the Church). You have already taken a bold step by adopting these artificial twins, but please, set yourself free and go the whole hog by letting them and the people around you know you adopted them. After all, you said you do not care anymore if anybody knows now. That is the way to true and lasting joy and peace with yourself, others around you, and even God, our Maker. Know also that these children might still see the truth someday, somehow. So, do not make the mistake of allowing them to discover the truth themselves after you're dead and gone or on your death bed. You must settle this crucial issue as soon as possible.

UNPROFITABLE RELATIONSHIP 2:
MY HUSBAND INSULTS ME OVER MY BODY

I got married about five years ago and was blessed with two sons. Before marriage, we engaged in premarital sex, so my husband cannot say he did not see my body before coming into the marriage. I am not particular about looks or body, but I try to look good as much as possible. If you check my pictures, I am a knockout any day!

After I had my first child, I noticed that my husband started passing some comments about the pointed breasts of women. There was a day he said some women still had their breasts in pointed shape, even after four children. I told him that is how God created them, and it is not of their own making. He said how come my breasts have fallen irredeemably and that he never enjoyed my breasts ever since we got married. He told me my vagina is ... He used to say so many horrible things about me anytime we quarrelled. He even told me once that I must have used charms on him because he never imagined he could settle for an expired *old woman* like me in the guise of a young girl.

I swear with the graves of my father and mother that I was not wayward before marriage or before meeting him. I had sexual relationships with only three or four men before meeting him. I made love to three of them, maybe once or twice each. I dated one man for over five years because I thought that was the guy I would marry until I noticed that his mother was against me. That was the only relationship where I would say I had much sex. I could not force myself into that marriage. He was the guy who deflowered me. I left him, and seven months later, the next man to come after him was a hit and run. We made love only once. The second man that came after six months was a loafer who had no job and no direction in life. He was posing with his father's car and had friends in top places.

He was not my kind of man. So I left him. I think we made love twice before I knew his true colours.

The last guy I met was in a Church. How did that happen? I cannot even say. We made love (was that even love?) ... in his car. I think I was just careless, and it is a thing I will regret all the days of my life. These were the men in my life.

Some women have even lost count of the men they had it with. When I met my husband, I told him about my life history. How my father and mother died in a motor accident when coming to see me at the university; how I matured overnight to become the mother of my siblings; how several men came in the guise of being helpers but with ulterior motives to take me to bed; how God saved me from a needless relationship and from falling victim to men due to fending for my siblings, how my father's boss adopted us and trained all of us; stood for us as a father, and his wife as our mother. He financed my wedding also. I disclosed all these to my husband.

I thought I would find a 'father' in him, but that was not to be. Anytime we had a little quarrel, all he would remember was my past; how loose I was to have been slept with in a car, how three men have used me like rainwater, such that my breasts had fallen. Is it wrong for a woman to reveal her past to her husband? I did, and I am regretting it today.

I know my body. Ever since I started growing breasts, mine had never been firm nor pointed. I explained this to him, but, during any quarrel, he would attack my body, lamenting that he had not enjoyed the wife of his youth. I am a loving wife. I am not dull in bed. I have created a happy home for him and my children. Now I am scared whenever it is closing time, and he returns home. Whenever he wants to make love, it is one abuse or the other, which kills my emotion.

I have not been able to take any action or confide in anybody because who will I speak with, except God? This man is killing me silently with these insults. He is injuring my sensibilities. I went through pains early in life. I thought I would have a happy home when I get married but this is what I get. I do not know how to handle this. Is it a mistake to reveal one's past to her husband? No one warned me. Perhaps my mum would have counselled me on marriage matters if she had lived long enough.

COUNSEL:

It was not wrong for you to have revealed your past to your husband but did he share his history also? There is no doubt that your husband is nagging because he is fantasizing about the bodies of other women outside the marriage. You need to be praying for him earnestly so he does not fall into adultery soon. Although you said you are not dull in be, there is much more to sex than being a mere physical activity. It is emotional and psychological too.

You will need to enhance your general physical outlook, especially in the regions he complains about. Please, maintain good hygiene and avoid wearing dull or drab clothes around the house as a general rule. Make sure you wear very nice perfumes that will attract him—wearing sexy lingerie and tight bras to make your breasts firm will also help. Ordinarily, a woman's breasts after having children will no longer be as firm or pointed if not enhanced with certain types of bras. You can talk to other women about this, especially those who know a lot about cosmetology and body enhancement. No sacrifice is too much to make to save your marriage. Please, do not give up!

UNPROFITABLE RELATIONSHIP 3:

HAVE I MADE A MISTAKE? CAN I BACK OUT?

I got married last year. I cannot say so far so good because of the recent developments. I am beginning to wonder if the voice of the people is not the voice of God, after all.

I am from Kogi State, he is from Edo. I noticed that right from the time I was dating him, my friends had reservations about his state of origin. They asked me why did I settle for an Edo guy? Do I not know them? I have heard so many people say negative things about guys from this state.

To me, there is nothing wrong with Edo state. I hate these sentiments and ethnic profiling. No state is bad. We can marry anywhere. Morality depends on the individual. As we have bad Edo guys, we have bad Kogi, Kwara, Lagos, Kaduna guys. There are millions of Edo guys who are morally balanced. That is my position, and I would marry him.

One day at a park in Abuja, my elder sister was travelling with me to Benin. The driver was cleverly asking her why would I marry an Edo man, adding that he is from the place and only Edo matches Edo or Delta people. I was sad when my sister retorted, 'We have warned her, but it's like the guy has used Benin *juju* (charms) on her'.

During our wedding reception, the chairman, whom my family invited, asked something like... 'since when did you know your husband?'. He stressed it like
'do-you-knooooooow-him?' He repeatedly asked me, and I got the message even though the guests were laughing.

After my wedding, some of my friends who saw my pictures on Facebook and Instagram were happy for me. But when they realised that I married an Edo guy, I noticed that their enthusiasm died down.

They asked me if there were no guys in Kogi or Kwara or... They always have these reservations!

This matter has started bothering me now because I found out some things about my husband. He has only a polytechnic diploma, and he lied to me that he read Business Administration from the University of Benin. What he claimed to be earning as salary was a lie. He is working with a forged Master's Degree certificate. I just found out and kept it to myself. I wonder how many shockers I will still face in this marriage. I am wondering if I was stupid after all!

Our marriage is almost a year old. I observed that he is clever at work, constantly engaging in some antics that I frown at. I keep telling him that God will not answer our prayers if he, the head of the house, is playing smart always. If I complain, he would say what he is doing is *runs,* and Edo guys are endowed to do it by nature. He would say, 'it is in our blood.' 'It is in our blood.' Those are his words...

We had a heated argument over the boy who hid in

a plane from Benin to Lagos. To me, the boy is a criminal. To my husband, he is smart. He even justified it that Adams Oshiomhole, the Governor of the state, gave the boy a big kudos, saying that in Edo state, you are born to be smart.

Now, I do not even know the difference between crime and being smart. My husband sees nothing wrong with his sisters loafing around in Italy. Our house is full of so many company properties he brought home. If I complain, he would say *dia fada,* (to hell with them), *nothing go happen,* and that he is doing everything to satisfy me.

I am not pregnant yet. Is opting out of this marriage at this stage a sin? Is it necessary? Is the voice of the people not the voice of God now? Was I wrong to have married him?

COUNSEL:

The problem with your husband is his relationship with God and not his state of origin. I agree with you that morality is an individual thing. You sound pretty religious yourself, but I am not sure you are born again because if you were, you would not have been married to an unbeliever against the warning of the word of God in the first place (2Corinthians 6: 14-18). But now, the deed is done! Opting out of your marriage is not the solution; God hates divorce (Malachi 2: 16; Matthew 19: 6; Romans 7: 2). If you opt out of this marriage, do you know what will happen in the next one? The Bible says, "And we know that all things work together for good to them that love God, to them who are the called according to His purpose" (Romans 8: 28). If you love God and call upon Him in prayers, He will show you mercy and change your husband. God can still use our mistakes to redirect us into His will, plans, and purpose for our lives, but it may take some time and not happen overnight. So, you need prayer and patience. Please, continue to pray for your husband, talk to him while you trust God, and wait patiently for Him to touch and change him.

UNPROFITABLE RELATIONSHIP 4: I AM GETTING FED UP WITH MY HUSBAND'S MONKEY BUSINESS

I am so encouraged by the last lady who wrote in on her husband. I also have a similar experience. This is my eighth year in marriage with no child.

Early last year, someone took us to a prophet who told us that my husband's hands are full of sins. He said my husband has made many people cry. That God wants him to clean himself up before he could answer us. The man did not take one penny from us.

To my husband, the prophet is a liar. He says he is only doing *runs*, hustling to survive, and doing that is no crime, as long as he does not kill anybody. I wept bitterly when we got home, asking him if he had ever killed. It became a big problem that I had to abandon the topic.

Let me give you some examples of his monkey business. As a senior staff in a shipping company, he has an official car. If the company replaces the old tyres of the vehicle with new ones, my husband will exchange the new tyres of the official vehicle for the old tyres of his car. He knows how to siphon fuel from his official vehicle into his car.

There is a wireless radio used in his office. Once my husband has it on him, he has a way of making people think he is a security official and to make them fear him. He would take a ride on commercial motorcycles (*okada*), and the *okada* riders would take him for a police officer in mufti, and they would dare not ask him for the fare. My husband has never paid *okada* riders in the last two years that he got the radio.

What about NEPA? He bypassed the prepaid meter by having an alternative wire that powers all the house's air conditioners, the electric cooker, deep freezers, pumping machine, and washing machine. He also engaged a technician to combine GOTV and

DSTV on the same dish, and we watched the pay TVs free! Close to our house is a company using Wi-Fi. We get their signals regularly. How my husband got their password still baffles me. He offered to connect my phone to the Wi-Fi, but I declined subtly.

I have known him with these dubious attitudes even before our marriage. Anytime I speak against it, he would say he will soon stop. He just wants to build on his wealth to establish himself. Nine years into the marriage, he is still doing this monkey business.

In his shipping company, it is against the rule to seek favours from the ship crew, but my husband will always seek, even blackmail them. When the shipping business was lucrative before the government of President Muhammadu Buhari stopped the importation of many goods, you needed to see what my husband brought home. If I complained, he would say I should call the police to arrest him. Now, I am tired of talking and warning him about the prophet's message that his hands are full of sins.

My husband does so many monkey businesses that violate our Christian faith, but he sees nothing wrong in them. He sees nothing wrong with those bursting pipelines or kidnapping. He would say they are collecting their share of the national cake.

If we are praying at home and I am praying against the enemies of Nigeria, my husband will stand up. He would say I am talking rubbish. Now, we do not pray together again. I told him that no prayer said in our house could be answered due to his lifestyle. I have a corner in my shop where I pray and ask God for intervention.

After eight years in a man's house, where can I go now? If people ask me why I left, what should I say? The prophet told me until my husband's hands are clean before I can be pregnant. And this is a man who cannot do without monkey business. I want God to direct me on what to do because I am getting fed up.

COUNSEL:

Your case is similar to that of the previous lady. Please, read the counsel I gave her: "The problem with your husband is his relationship with God and not his state of origin. Morality is an individual thing. You sound pretty religious yourself, but I am not sure you are born again because if you were, you would not have married an unbeliever against the word of God in the first place (2Corinthians 6: 14-18), but now the deed is done. Opting out of your marriage is not the solution; God hates divorce (Malachi 2: 16; Matthew 19: 6; Romans 7: 2). If you opt out of this marriage, do you know what will happen in the next one? The Bible says, "And we know that all things work together for good to them that love God, to them who are the called according to His purpose" (Romans 8: 28). If you love God and call upon Him in prayers, He will show you mercy and change your husband. God can still use our mistakes to redirect us into His will, plans, and purpose for our lives, but it may take some time and not happen overnight. So, you need prayer and patience. Please, continue to pray for your husband and talk to him while you trust God and wait patiently for Him to touch and change your husband." Like this other lady, you married an ungodly man and a crook, but much more than the pressure to have children, your husband's salvation is urgent and should be paramount to you. You must be born again, too; being religious is not enough!

UNPROFITABLE RELATIONSHIP 5:
I AM MARRIED TO A SHE-MAN

My marriage is just eight years old. I have three children, twins (two girls), seven and a three-year-old boy. My husband is from the *Igbomina*-speaking area of Kwara state; his mother is Ijebu, and I am from Iseyin. If I had known that his mother was the kind of person she turned out to be, I would never have married my husband. Never and never!

I want to use this opportunity to warn single ladies that they would need to thoroughly check their husbands' families, their ability to be a man, who their mothers are, and where they come from. Yes, where they come from, and speak with the wives who married into the house before her on their experiences. If I had found someone to tell me these, I would not have married this she-man.

His mother is the head of the house. After getting into the family, I discovered that this Ijebu woman turned her husband into a weakling. His father had no say in the house. It is whatever she says. The children fear their mother more than their father. I am the fourth wife in the house. She has four boys and two girls. My husband is the last boy. He fears his mama more than God. If she is talking, my husband will put his hands at his back, looking down, just like their eldest brother in his late 40s. If my husband is making love to me and his mother's call comes in, his penis would shrink, and he would drive like a mad man to her place at Isolo from here. The woman picked the locations to reside for all her children, even our house. She would call any of her sons' wives to weave her hair.

All these shouldn't have been my problem. Not until her orders began to infringe on my life. She took over the naming ceremony when I had the twins as if I, the biological mother, had no say. She brought the names of the children without consulting my parents or me. Not even her husband said anything. The man was silent. When they brought the printed names, I asked my husband, 'why would your mother name my children and I, the mother would have no say?' I was ready to stop the ceremony. I took my children into the car and was prepared to drive away. It became a big issue. My parents were there but said nothing. After a while, they left. The Pastor prevailed that it was wrong for her to usurp the naming ceremony. That was when peace was established. The same thing happened at the naming ceremony of my boy. She was spoiled for a fight. My husband was just like a figurehead!

If this woman had a rift with her children, she would call all other children to boycott the offender, and 'no one should interact with him.' And that is what all of them would do. No one, I say no one would dare speak with the offender until they got clearance from their mother.

The wives who married into their family before me

could not do anything because the very first wife was afraid. So, the next wife, whom I jocularly call Wife 2, had no one to work with to defy mama's orders; same with the third wife, Wife 3. I am the 4th wife, a lone ranger.

The mama would call any wife on the phone to come and wash her clothes or cook for her. I heard these from all of them when we just got married. The first time she called me, I told her I was busy at the office. She cut the phone. My husband's phone rang the next minute, and I heard him saying, 'Yes, ma. Yes, ma. Yes, ma'. I thought he would come to me; I would have given him the sharpness of my tongue. That was the basis of my disagreement with the mother to date. I once told her that I am in charge in my husband's house, not any other woman, whoever she may be.

If I have any disagreement with my husband, the first person he would call is his mother. His mother would call me in less than five minutes and start talking, "you are badly trained. You have no home training. Your parents did not get it right." The day she mentioned my parents was the first day I told my husband that I was not scared of divorce. I would not be the first or the last. My bold stance has radicalized Wife 2 and Wife 3.

On January 2, 2015, she invited us to her home at Isolo, where we had a mini party. I did not eat anything because I did not trust her. I only drank wine. After the party, she sat us down and read her wishes for 2016. What caught my attention was when she said at *Ileya* festive period, we would all follow her to Ijebu. I was the first to ask why. I told her I am a Christian and my husband is one. What is our business with *Ileya*? She said that was the tradition of all Ijebu people, Christian or Muslim.

Wife 2 now said only her husband could take her there because she knows nobody there. My husband does not go there ordinarily. He is not an *Ojude Oba* person. And so, I also told his mother that only my husband could instruct me on where to go. She got angry, stood up, and called her children. The firstborn and my husband had disappeared. Only Husbands 2 and 3 were there. They said nothing.

On January 4, she came to my house and said I should start packing. My marriage was over with her son. My husband sat there watching. I did not respond to her until the two boys she brought were told to pack my luggage into my bedroom. And they entered my bedroom. That was when I went off. I created a scene with them and a bigger scene with her. I went into my bedroom and pushed her out. I called the police that an intruder was here. I told her to get out of my home. That was how my husband began to beat me that I was pushing his mum. I called my brothers and parents, and they all came. The scene became worse, after which the police came and told her that she had trespassed and could be arrested. That was when she left with the boys. I told my parents I was ready to move out. They moved my things out of the house. I moved the two cars in the house, which I bought, and my children. I am now back at my parent's house.

My husband did not call me until much later, asking where I was. I cut the phone. When he called again, I told him that I would not have married him if I knew he was such a bastard. I told him to stop calling me. I am sure his mama has told other children to boycott him.

Sincerely, I am not scared of divorce. A few days after, Wife 2 and 3 came here to visit me and said they were also ready for the woman. I do not care if they are or not. I care for my peace in my husband's home.

Where do I go from here?

COUNSEL:

The deed is done, and thank God your marriage is also blessed with three children. It is good for others to learn from your story. Nothing is wrong with the tribe of your mother-in-law, but something is seriously wrong with her personality and

character; she is hugely domineering! You have either of two options: you can return to your husband's house and resume resisting your mother-in-law until she is overwhelmed and gives up on your home (James 4: 7) or, you remain on your own and continue to live with your children as a single mother provided you can remain unmarried for the rest of your life. Either way, you must be powerful and prayerful. And one major lesson for you is to give your children and their spouses their well-deserved space and respect their privacy later on in life when they are married. Now, you are the accuser. Then, you could become the accused. Make sure you do not do to your daughters-in-law what your mother-in-law is doing to you.

UNPROFITABLE RELATIONSHIP 6: MY SUNDAY SCHOOL TEACHER'S WIFE SLEEPS AROUND

I am concerned about this matter because whoever sees evil and does not react against it is cooperating with it. I am a Christian, and we need to be our brothers' keepers.

In Yoruba land, we believe that if a wife is engaging in adultery, such a woman can kill her husband, and I believe that the adultery of a wife has a significant repercussion on the husband and the children. That is why I took an interest in this matter and decided to forward all the details to you to advise me on what to do.

I work in a big hotel around Sango, and I am a

member of *XYZ* Church. I live in Alakuko where my Church is based. One day in September 2015, a woman I recognised as the wife of my Sunday school teacher came to our hotel with a man. I was shocked to see her being led to one of the rooms. This year alone, I have seen her in this hotel more than fifteen times. I know the man very well. He is a lawyer and well-to-do. His phone number is 080..... and the car registration number is ...... The name of the woman is Mrs. .... *(The vital information edited out).* Find attached the pictures that I snapped each time they came to lodge in the hotel.

The first or second time I saw her, I thought I was mistaken. I observed her closely the following Sunday and confirmed that she was the one. She does not know me, but I know her because of her loud manners in Church. You could take her for an angel. I always pity her husband, who consistently portrays his wife as a virtuous woman.

The husband was well to do, but the economy is affecting him now. I would not know why this woman is doing this. There was a weekend she came into the hotel with a piece of luggage, and I knew she came to lodge for the weekend. The following Sunday, I heard my Sunday school teacher telling her friends that she went to Ekiti for a burial ceremony of her friend. The woman was in our hotel. I attached some receipts of their lodgings to show you that I am not lying. You can see the disguised name of the man.

Every Sunday, I feel for this man. I think I am doing him an enormous disservice by keeping quiet. There was a time I felt like writing all I knew and sneaking it into his car, but I feared I could be traced. I also wanted to send text messages to his number to come and catch her red-handed anytime she was around, but I am troubled about it.

I wanted to discuss this matter with my wife, but I know women cannot keep secrets. Yet, I do not want God to hold me responsible for any evil that may happen to this man. I have proof, as you can see that his wife is unfaithful. I feel so jealous of this godly man. What do you advise me to do? Should I just keep quiet or find a way of telling the husband? Or can you help me dispatch the details to the husband? What should be a Christian's attitude to a matter like this?

NK.

COUNSEL:

With the loads of evidence you have, you are already an accomplice in this woman's sins, and God will hold you responsible for your action or inaction (Ezekiel.3: 17-21; James 4: 17). You should confide the details (with proofs) of these woman's adultery in your Pastor, who has spiritual oversight of her and her husband more so that the husband is a Sunday School teacher in the Church. That way, you will absolve yourself of any complicity in the matter and shift the whole responsibility to your pastor. Your pastor's subsequent action or inaction will show him as a godly Pastor or otherwise. He is accountable after that before God.

UNPROFITABLE RELATIONSHIP 7: IF SUNDAY SCHOOL TEACHER IS OF GOD, HOLY SPIRIT WILL EXPOSE WIFE

I read the story of the hotel attendant who saw the wife of his Sunday school teacher, and I congratulate him as a good Christian. If we have no sin in our hearts, we will not be comfortable with sin anywhere we see it. I was distraught when I read many reactions, especially of ladies calling the man *Amebo* (talebearer). I understand the drift of Mr. Bola Adewara that he should leave the man to discover who his wife is himself. That is a good one. That is why I decided to tell the story of my marriage, how my marriage crumbled five years ago, how the Holy Spirit saved me, how I nearly ran mad and how God has redeemed me and settled me with a better woman.

I was warned not to marry this lady, but I went ahead. She is from one of the popular towns in Ogun State, reputed to be wayward party lovers. I will not mention any town, but the initiated will know it. I became a born again Christian after our marriage. Tinuke would tell me she was going to parties in her town. Every weekend, she attended one party or the other. Yes, we always attended parties before we got married, but I slowed down after, and I tried to slow her down too, but it was difficult. She had friends, numerous friends from the same town. Her mother is a divorcee. I should have known that they could not change.

The first sign I noticed was that my wife would put off her phones when we were together, and they were always with her. I could not use them when I had no airtime on mine. If she left the phones on the table, it was always in silence and pass-worded. I became suspicious. Who was she running from? When I asked her, she would say they were some of her female friends. We had so many issues like that. I was no longer comfortable with her in the house at a stage. My spirit became troubled, and when I slept on the same bed with her, it was like the Spirit was telling me that my wife was dubious. I had a great foreboding in my spirit. I never knew it was the Holy Spirit in me.

The countdown began when I began to pray, asking God to reveal what I did not know about my wife. Brethren, there is no greater *Amebo* than the Holy Spirit. He is a discerner of all minds and spirits. He will teach us all things as Jesus said. ALL THINGS, if we are faithful with Jesus.

One day I was in the sitting room, and my wife was dressing, as usual, ready to go out. She said she wanted to visit her friend in the hospital. She hadn't notified me before. She just told me about 30 minutes back and started dressing up. I did not say a word as I sat in the sitting room. Soon after, I felt it in my spirit to go and eavesdrop on her by the door to the bedroom. But I felt what for? I was too busy. But the Spirit moved me unusually. And I found myself moving mechanically towards the bedroom. The Spirit diverted me to go outside and stand by the windows of the bedroom. That was what I did, and I heard my wife fixing an appointment with someone to come to a particular junction, a bit far from our house and wait there. I wanted to go inside and confront her, but the Spirit said no, trace her to the bus stop.

When she was done with her dressing, she came out, gave me a peck like a loving wife (WOMEN!), and said she would soon be back. I was boiling inside, but I pretended not to bother. She took a bike and, when I saw the bike had gone far, I took another bike and followed her. She was far ahead of me. She got to the junction, alighted, and walked towards a car parked near a taxi park. I have so many friends there.

As I alighted from my *Okada*, I saw her entering the car, and I heard the Spirit telling me to move in. I walked brusquely to her, and I said: "Tinuke, but you told me you were going to the hospital. Is this how to be a good wife?"

I folded my hands on my head and began to ... I am now ashamed to say I wept. The taxi drivers heard me shouting, "Haa! Tinuke, Haa! Tinuke Haa!" As friends, they came to me to ask what had happened. Four of them surrounded the car, brought the man out, and pounced on him. The beating was so much. The more I persuaded them to leave him alone, the more the beating continued. They removed his clothes, cut some branches of a tree, and gave him several lashes right there in my presence. He was weeping and shouting for mercy. My wife had disappeared, typical of women when the crunch comes. I also moved away. I did not want a court case. I would not know what happened to that guy eventually. I stopped passing through that road out of shame till I moved out of that area. That was the last day I saw my wife. Six months later, her mother came. I mean six months later! She said she came to apologise. See who I called a mother-in-law? Anyway, I thank my Church members for standing by me. I almost ran mad, but they stood by me.

After the sad event, my first challenge was how to cope with the three children. Recently, their mother attempted to reach them through one of her friends in the Church. I cannot and would not stop her from seeing them. However, I have remarried since, and the bitterness of the past is gone. I have two other children now from a godly wife. Praise the living God!

The gist of my story is that the Sunday school teacher needs to pray and ask God to show him who his wife is. God is not a man that He should lie nor the son of man that He should repent. If we truly know God, no *Amebo* is greater than the Holy Spirit. He will always reveal the secrets of life to us.

COUNSEL:

Yes, the Holy Spirit reveals secrets

(Deuteronomy 29: 29; Daniel 2: 47), but He is not an Amebo or busybody (1Peter 4: 15) as you erroneously presented Him. That is grossly misleading and disrespectful of God. If you were that prayerful and close to God as you claimed, why did not you pray to God to reveal your wife's character to you before marrying her? God still hates divorce, and divorcees are people who should not serve in Church leadership lest they constitute bad examples and contaminate God's people and work (1 Timothy 3: 2 & 12; Titus 1: 6). It is better to seek God's help to lay a firm foundation for our marriage in the first place than seek Him later to mend or repair it when we are in hot soup, and things start falling apart. However, better late than never!

UNPROFITABLE RELATIONSHIP 8: WHAT ELSE DOES MY WIFE WANT?

My home is on fire, stoked by my wife and partly by me. She led me into it. Although I am ashamed now to disclose what I did, as I said, she pushed me into it. One night, after so many months of doing it, she caught me right on top of a lady she brought home as her cousin.

That girl was wayward from the first day she came into our house. This girl would not wear a bra, her pointed nipples protruding from whatever she wears. I had told my wife to take care of her. Whenever my friends came to our house, they discreetly passed some comments, but my wife did not know that the girl was causing some commotions around us guys.

Now, my wife is the genesis of her problems. She

always came up with one excuse or the other. As for me, I am very virile and sexually active. I used to have girlfriends but not anymore. At least, I controlled myself. This lady, a polytechnic graduate waiting to go on national service, would talk provocatively when watching Yoruba films. I had caught her a few times watching pornographic movies on my laptop.

One day, I picked her Samsung phone... she had so many porno movies on them. Before I knew it, my mind was drawn to her. This lady would call me during office hours to bring my food or need something. I always wondered why she would not call her sister. One day she came to my office under the pretext of going to the market and was short of money. I took her out for lunch, and... one thing led to the other, and we made love inside the car at a remote corner at the back of my office. That was how she came every day. This girl was a bomb. I got free from her what my wife could not give easily.

At home, anytime my wife refused my sexual

advances and slept off, I had a way of standing up in the middle of the night under the guise of visiting the loo and would end up in this girl's room to do a quickie and return to bed. I confess that I have done this several times. She had aborted once and told me she had aborted three times before.

I would not know how it happened that day, but my wife caught me right on top of her. I was shocked. Life went out of me. My wife did not say anything till now. And she did not cry. I have not seen her touched by the revelation. When I returned home the second day after we were caught, the lady had left the house. That evening, I heard my wife discussing on the phone, saying something like, "I thought I was helping you and your daughter. I told my husband that we were cousins. I do not know you people from Adam. We only lived together as neighbours in Ibadan. Now, Folashade has done this to me. *E seun o*. Thank you." She cut the line when I entered. I prostrated to explain; she just brushed me aside and went out into the kitchen.

Every day she would prepare the food for the house, but there were no discussions between us. I wanted to open a line of communication to apologize to her, but she did not give me a chance. I know I have offended my darling wife, but she led me into it. She would not sleep in bed with me. She would sleep on the sofa in the sitting room even till now. She would greet me in the morning; take care of the three children. She still gives me food, but I am afraid to eat. I always sanctify the food before eating. You cannot trust women on issues like these. I have been seeking lines of communication with her daily, but she blocks me.

I went to the Church to seek forgiveness with God and made a vow that this would be the last time it would happen. I felt within my heart that God had forgiven me. Why is my wife crucifying me? I have not heard this matter from anybody, none of her friends. She stopped using the family cars, preferring to board public transport. I bought her so many things, I have spent over fifty thousand naira on things, but she brushed them aside. My home is stiff and hot. Everywhere is quiet. No conversation. I am dying inside. My problem is how do I break the silence? I want her to talk with me. A friend I confided in said I should use boldface or *shakara* her or *ogboju*. But it is like putting petrol in a fire. My wife has no spirit of God in her; she is just claiming to be a church worker. If she is genuinely born again, why would she not forgive and open lines of communication to explain my side of the story? It is three months now!

Look at what she did again: last week I went to her office to see if she would talk to me. I bought some items for her. Immediately she saw me, she greeted me nicely as her loving husband, introduced me to all her friends as "my darling husband." She spoke to me so well, so proudly as if nothing was wrong. I was shocked. I said, women! I sat with her for 30 minutes. Any issue I raised, she discussed politely. When I tried to go to the main problem, she walked away. She saw me off when I took my leave, and her friends envied us as 'love birds.' When we got home, she switched off. It was like she was not the same woman I met in her office.

I do not know if you should publish this story because some women would be too quick to vent their anger on me as if they do not make mistakes. They should hold their peace! No one should abuse me. God has not condemned me. He says I should go and sin no more. So, how do I break this silence? How can I beg her? How can I appeal to a woman that is deeply hurt? After all, no one is above mistakes!

COUNSEL:

Please, stop justifying yourself! I am sure the lady in question did not hold your shirt or drag you into bed with her. Joseph was strong and virile like you, yet, he called what you have done "great wickedness" (Genesis 39: 9). You have hurt your wife beyond words, and you cannot be the Judge and Plaintiff in your case at the same time. You need to be broken and truly develop godly sorrow, which works out repentance in the first place (2Corinthians 7: 10), and not resort to boldface, shakara, or ogboju like some of your friends wrongly counselled you. Trying to cover up or justify yourself will only worsen a lousy matter (Proverbs 28: 13); only genuine remorse and repentance will help your case. Eventually, according to Proverbs 16: 7, when your ways please God, He will make your wife be at peace with you. That is a significant way to ascertain God's forgiveness and not just be presumptuous.

UNPROFITABLE RELATIONSHIP 9: MOTHERS, WATCH IT

Several weeks ago, I got a message in my inbox from a lady who said she needed to see me in person to discuss her daughter. I did not know her, but when she introduced herself as one of my readers who has been following me for years and mentioned some of my old posts, I gave her my address. In a few minutes, she was outside my house in her Sienna car with an elderly woman, likely to be in her late 40s. When she told me her story briefly, I agreed to follow her home to see the pregnant 14-year-old daughter.

Her husband works outside Lagos. She is a civil servant, and she is managing two barbing salons and three commercial buses her husband bought for her. When the drivers of the buses close for the day and bring the buses home, they often sit at the barber's shop in front of their building. There, they drink and are merry with friends.

Her first daughter, a 14-year-old student, often mixed with them because the drivers and barbers remit their money to her. According to her, she has no reason to suspect them since they all knew her age and knew she was in school. The barbers and the drivers treat her like their sister.

Some time ago, she told her mum that she did not see her menses at the end of the month. The mother said it could be *jedijedi* (Pile) and gave her a native concoction called *Oroki*. By Good Friday, menses did not surface. She decided to take her to the hospital. She got the rudest shock of her life... her daughter was two months pregnant. She said she fainted.

Back home, questions and answers followed. The young girl confessed that Bashiru, the Ibadan-born driver, did it. And since then, she refused to reveal any more information hence the mother's decision to call me. She would not want anybody or neighbours to hear of this. I now sent for the daughter.

She is a pretty dark-complexioned girl. Her stature is big for her age. She was fully breasted and seemed like an 18-year old. I am sure most guys would be confused about her age. I told the mother to excuse us so I could speak with her privately.

"What did you see in Bashiru? You love him?"

"No."

"Then why did you allow him to sleep with you?"

No response.

"Is he the first man to sleep with you?

"Yes."

"When?"

"Last year."

"Last year? When you were just 13?"

No response.

"What does Bashiru do for you?"

"He gives me money and buys things for me. And he advises me too like his sister. He talks to me gently."

"What does he buy for you?"

"Meat pie, doughnuts, ice cream, recharge cards, internet airtime."

"Does your mum not buy them for you?"

She was quiet, tears dripping down her cheeks.

"How many times has he slept with you?"

"I cannot count it."

"Once a week? Twice a month?"

No response

"Where does he make love to you?"

"Inside the bus."

"You sleep on the seats inside the bus..."

"Yes. Or he will say I should bend down by the side of the bus in darkness."

"Did he force you, rape you?"

No response.

I collected her phone and, scanning through the pictures, I saw her nude photos, boobs, cunts, penis (of course, Bashiru's), and some porn films. From her phone, I noticed that she is on *Facebook, Whatsapp, Instagram, Pinit*, and some other social media that I don't know.

I asked the mother if she often checks her phone. "No," she said. She does not.

"Why did you buy a phone for an SS1 student?"

"Her father did." Time to shift blame! I gave the phone to her to go through. She did. She could not look at me in the eyes again.

"Madam, your laxity led to this problem."

"Uncle B," she said apologetically, almost inaudibly. "Are you blaming me now?"

"I am not just blaming you. If I have a cane, I will give you twelve lashes for parental negligence. Your daughter has been sexually active long ago. She has been way-ward more than you can imagine, yet she is just 14!"

Anyway, she resolved to get an abortion for her, but most hospitals she went to, according to her, said they do not do it.

Now listen to this funny one: One of the reasons she called me was to see if I could help her get a good doctor who would be well paid. I laughed. The pregnancy is fast running into the third month.

She wants to punish Bashiru severely. She is ready to do anything to make Bashiru stew in his juice. But her fears are "if I confront Bashiru that he impregnated my daughter, he could insist that he would be responsible for the pregnancy and nothing must happen to it. Where do I go with that, with a daughter so naive to have slept with a tout?"

Also, while dealing with Bashiru, her husband could get to know her. And the threats of him closing the shops and selling off the buses are certain. The father must not hear that a bus conductor or driver impregnated his daughter. She would not accept that her daughter's ordeal was essentially her fault.

I tried to advise her against abortion. She then asked me a question I could not answer immediately: "Uncle B, if your daughter is pregnant for a Lagos bus driver or conductor, would you have done an abortion for her or not?"

COUNSEL:

It is worthless crying over spilt milk. Prevention is better than cure; it is better to be safe than be sorry. Why do some people fear men more than God; why don't parents do all that is needful in training their children and giving them sound sex education to prevent this mess but prefer to be later running here and there looking for ungodly quick fixes. It is bad enough for a teenage girl to be pregnant, but it is worse for the mother to want to procure an abortion for her. She fornicated, but the mother now wants to commit murder! Carrying Bashiru's baby is not the same thing as marrying Bashiru. The girl should be allowed to carry her pregnancy to term and deliver the baby while Bashiru takes care, but she does not have to marry him. The reproach therein is punishment for the parents for their negligence and punishment for the girl for her naivety and fornication. Good, godly home training and sound sex education are the only sure way to avoid such reproach, especially for our adolescents.

UNPROFITABLE RELATIONSHIP 10:

BORN AGAIN CHRISTIAN MARRIED TO A MUSLIM

I am pondering how to spend this year with Christ, my family, and I. But there is a stumbling block, hence my decision to get in touch with you.

I am 42 and still a struggling civil servant. I became a born-again Christian two years ago, and I should be enjoying Christ better than we are in my home. However, we thank God for what he has done for us so far.

When I met my wife almost 14 years ago, she was a Muslim, and I was just a nominal Christian. Her father was the Imam of a famous mosque here in Lagos. He opposed her marriage to a Christian, but her mother loved me and supported me in marrying her on the condition that I agree with the family that I would allow her to continue with her religion, and under no conditions would I force her into Christianity. The mother said my wife is a significant child to them, and it was because of her that her father promised Allah to build a mosque if God gave her, the mother and first wife, a child after 15 years of marriage. And when God answered, he built the mosque. So nothing could turn that child away from Islam.

At that time, I was ready for any eventualities to have my wife. I agreed with them, and the father said some things, giving me the Koran to hold, that if I changed that agreement *this and that* will happen to me, his daughter, and all the children she might bear for me. He died five years ago. But the mother is still alive.

I became a born-again Christian two years ago, and I am like a Pastor in my Church. I do not need to go into the distress that brought me to Christ. Uncle Bola, I went through pains, and I know that only Jesus can save.

When I gave my life to Christ, my wife supported me

but said I should allow her to practice her religion as agreed. I have been coping with the family of the bondwoman ever since. Now, this is affecting me in my Church, as some of the youths I pastor keep saying if Pastor X could marry a Muslim, they too could. They see my marriage as a tacit endorsement of "we are all worshipping the same God." That is also what my wife says, but we as Christians know that we are not worshipping the same God as the Muslims.

My wife is not ready to follow me into Christianity. She is so encouraged by her mother and siblings. They keep referring me to the agreement between their late father and I. I have discussed with some Muslims who told me that Islam permits their women to adapt to the religion of their husbands. But why is my wife's family holding on to an agreement that holds no water, an arrangement I made just to pick my wife.

This issue is ongoing in my house. My Church will not promote me to be a full Pastor until I sort out myself in this area. I have been in prayers over this matter, and I want you to pray with me. Do I need to change Church? I love my wife, and she loves me. But she says it is not in her powers to renounce Islam since I agreed with her father, using the Koran. I did this when I did not know the implications.

COUNSEL:

You sure need prayer and patience to overcome this challenge though it appears as if you're primarily concerned about your promotion and public perception as a Pastor in your Church than the salvation of your wife. You need a genuine change of attitude to experience divine intervention in this matter, but it is a small thing before God, "For with God nothing shall be impossible" (Luke 1: 37). But you must pray for your wife sincerely and be patient.

UNPROFITABLE RELATIONSHIP 11: THE RUBBISH WE CALL LOVE AFFAIR!

SHE: I am a single mother of two children, 15 and 13 years old. Their father and I got separated about nine years ago, and since then, he has not been helpful. The reason for our separation is a different story entirely. I am not concerned with that here.

About five years ago, I met a man that I believed would be my joy since that was what I had been praying for. I embraced him, showered him with all my love and respect. I also changed my phone number for him to know that I did not want to live in the past again. I surrendered all to him, even my whole body. I gave him my old sim card to destroy, but he kept it and selected some numbers he suspected on it, and started calling them to ask about their relationships with me. Thank God I do not have a skeleton in my cupboard. I got to know later and felt terrible about it because that was not our agreement. We talked it over because he assists me with the upkeep of the children.

At the initial stage, I loved him so much, thinking we were going to get married, but I had to soft-pedal when I saw the way he complained about his wife. He's troublesome. He fights with my friends, both males, and females. He hacked my Facebook password, entered and selected the names of some friends, and started sending abusive messages to them and calling them names. He got their numbers online; he called or sent Whatsapp messages.

There is no day he would not fight with me. He would abuse me, talk to me as if I should go and die, and make me cry bitterly. All I enjoy from him now is money, no more love. I do not even enjoy lovemaking with him, but I do it to please him. I cannot even tell anyone that I am a single mother because he would know. I am 42 years old, a junior public servant. Would I remain like this for life? Can you please post it on your wall?

BOLA: I will. But there are questions I need to ask before posting. The story is not exhaustive. What happened with your first husband?

SHE: I said it is a whole story itself. He's a Muslim, while I am a Christian. It is a family problem. My dad (now late) initially opposed the marriage. He later agreed when I insisted. My former husband promised to allow me to practice my religion. Sometimes, he followed me to Church during special programmes, but his father and some family members were chronic Muslims who put up a big fight which I fought for sometimes before I gave up. They wanted me to get converted to Islam, but I refused. Initially, he supported me, but things changed later. Also, he is not educated. Still, I managed to carry him along, but he does not have a good family. Maybe they thought I was going to take him away from them. I later learnt that his mother went through the same route. She, a Christian was pregnant with him (my former husband) for his dad, but his grandfather did not accept her, so they took him away from her at just six months!

BOLA: *O ga o!* This life *sha*! This rubbish called love affair!

SHE: *Na so we see am o*. Hope you understand my message *sha*? Ask questions where it is not clear.

BOLA: I do. I will post.

SHE: Please, do not mention my name o.

BOLA: *Haba!* I *be baby now*? *Sebi I still dey suck breast ...lol*

SHE: When are you going to post it?

BOLA: Shortly. I have so many cases like this on my hand that I have not treated. You will please be patient. But I can do *ojoro* by posting yours quickly because of the urgency.

SHE: Alright. I am ok.

COUNSEL:

Let's face facts! Are you sure the man you are going out with now is not married and have a family of his own somewhere at his age? The fact that he is now so jealous and abusive is another point that should make you think twice about the relationship. Your primary point of attraction in the relationship is the financial benefits you're deriving from this man who does not love you or care about your feelings. In business, it does not matter whatever the capital outlay may be, but once the losses are more than the gains, it is a bad business – straight and simple! Please, sit down again and ask yourself what you want out of this relationship more so that you are already a mother of two teenage boys.

UNPROFITABLE RELATIONSHIP 12:
FOR 24 YEARS, I NEVER KNEW MY FATHER

I graduated last year from Ogun State University, and I am now doing the national service in Enugu State. For everything, let me give kudos to my mom for my life, her selflessness, and doggedness at ensuring that I must be educated. I know what she went through to educate me. Many times she would sell her gold, clothes, etc., to raise money for me. I am her first child. I have two sisters after me from another father. My mother's marriages failed. I do not know why. But from my reading of her, she was just unlucky. She is not an evil woman morally. At least, I do not see her with men, and she is not the partying type. She reads a lot, and I know she is intelligent. She is a nurse. Her major problem is she is too self-opinionated. She is touchy when it comes to discussions about love or marriage. We live in a sparsely furnished room and a parlour in a face-me-I-face-you building in Bariga. We were not hungry, but we could live better. We did not go to the best schools, and we did not wear the best clothes.

I see my mates talk about their fathers and how they take them out. Never have I spoken about mine. It has always been my mom. And she was there for me. The first time I was hit by the absence of a father figure in my life was when I was to fill a form, and I got to the father's name and state of origin. All my life, mom has always filled my forms. While friends were waiting on me to finish filling out the form to go and submit it, I picked up my phone and called her. "What are my father's town and his profession". My mom was silent. Then she dropped the call. I called her again, and she ordered me to write that my father was late and that I am from Lagos State. I did that reluctantly. But the seed of discord and question was sown in me already.

When I got home that weekend, she knew I would bring up the issue. She was stiff and in no mood to entertain me. She took her face off me and pretended to be too busy and severe. I understood her, and she knew I knew the game. I also resolved to begin a series of actions that will lead to a discussion on my paternity someday. Can you imagine, I was over 22 years old then, and not once did she bring up the issue of my paternity? And I had taken it that way until the form issue.

When I returned to school, I sought an audience with a female lecturer in my department. The woman always gave me attention because I did well in her course. I told her my story, and she got angry about why I would be treated that way. She said I had the right to have a relationship with my father, and whatever could have happened between my mom and him was their issue and should be restricted to them.

She said my father too must be stupid for not searching for me but retreated immediately that he might have no clue about my whereabouts if my mom was hiding me from him. She said I must go home and tell her I wanted to speak with her about my paternity. If she attends to me, I should hear her out and let her know my mother's response.

Anytime I planned to raise the issue, courage would fail me. Whenever I got home and felt like raising the matter, it was like she always knew and would become stiff and resistant. One night, as we were about to sleep, I went to sit by her bed and said, “Mommy...”

Hurriedly, she interjected. “Don't come here and start asking me stupid questions. If you are not ready to sleep, go to the parlour and watch TV.” She then turned her back on me and covered herself up with her wrapper. I walked away like a whipped dog, but I knew the days were numbered.

When I got to school, I would dodge the lecturer. I could not tell her I was scared of my mum. One day, she was driving past, and she caught sight of me. I confessed to her. She said I could only die once. It was a Friday. I made up my mind I was going home right now. And to home, I went.

I was looking tough, and my mom knew something was on my mind. She knew it immediately she saw me and asked, "Yes, what is it?"

I said, "I want to meet my dad today."

"You are stupid," she said. "What do you need him for? When he was not here in the last 24 years, did you not live your life? Have you missed anything? Have I not tried my best as a mother? Is this how you want to pay me back for all my suffering and labour over you, Enitan, you ungrateful child! You must be a stupid girl. If you annoy me, I will curse you."

That was when I sparked. "No, mommy, I will not take that today. I want to know who my daddy is. I want to live like any other child. I am not a baby again. I am almost 24, but for my education, I am fit to get married." I was shouting and went outside the parlour to the corridor of the face-me-I-face-you apartments. "Mommy, today I want to know him. Today! I will not take this any longer. I am not a baby." I went on and on along the corridors...

The neighbours had gathered. A neighbour, an old man we called Baba Sayo came to me, told me to keep quiet, and together, we went inside to meet my mom. We met her weeping bitterly. I stood there for a while and later walked away. The baba came later to invite me in. When I saw my mom weeping and shivering, I felt I had hurt her. I began to weep and went on my knees before her. She held me, embraced me, and said, “Enny, you have opened a sad, old wound in my life. Sit down and let me speak with you.” She could not speak. She laid on the sofa quietly, tears rolling down the sides of her eyes. I heard her say, "I knew a day like this would come. I had feared this day."

At about eight pm, she felt composed to speak to me. We have separate beds in the bedroom, lying side by side. She sat up and told me stories. I wept. I wept for my mom. Evil things men do to women... I regret ever shouting at my mom. I never knew that was the story.

Two days later, I decided to find my dad in Abuja. She told me he works with the Federal Ministry of ... and his office is at the Federal Secretariat. I have never been to Abuja, but I was determined to go there. In her discussions with me, she said I looked every bit like him, same complexion, face, etc.

By 5 am, I stood up and began to pack a small bag. I did not tell her what I was doing. I was crazy. There were tension and anxiety all over me. It was a Friday morning. I wore a pair of jeans trousers and picked the bag. I knelt by her bed and told her I was going to Abuja to look for my dad. She said, "No way. You will do no such thing". I knew she would try to stop me. But no one dares Enny.

COUNSEL:

Dear Enny,

Congratulations on finally taking the bull by the horn to resolve the mystery behind your paternity. Though you did not share the conclusion of your story, at least you met your father eventually. That's a significant breakthrough! It is also some big lessons for women (or men in some cases) who wrongly believe they can take care of their children alone without any input from their spouse. No man or woman can have a child alone, so no man or woman should raise a child alone except the other person is dead. It is an unnecessary burden we should not bear. Even when one party is grossly irresponsible, we should not still deny the children access to them at some point as that will be a terrible injustice to those children, especially before they start to think of getting married. It is better to jaw-jaw than to war-war, and it is better to do so on time!

UNPROFITABLE RELATIONSHIP 13: HIS GENITAL IS AS SMALL AS MY INDEX FINGER

I have no sexual satisfaction in this marriage

I am two years old in marriage with no sexual satisfaction. The most considerable distress I have in all of this is that I was deceived into the marriage by that theory that says ‘no sex before marriage. I am not questioning God or the Bible. But I feel we need to define issues more clearly so that we do not get into trouble, the type I am in now.

I met my husband when we were doing our national service at Awka. He gave me a born again façade. I am also a Christian. Better still, a struggling Christian. I know Christ; I know what is correct and try to do them though I still miss my steps just like any other person, once in a while. I do not pester him for sex on account of our Christian faith. I know what the scriptures say about this.

We got married about eight months later. The first sign of the coming problem was that my husband would never be private with me throughout our courtship. He would never ask for sex nor try to arouse me. It is not as if I am a pervert who wants sex before marriage, but it is 'normal' to expect a dating guy to make moves, and the woman will object till the wedding day. This guy never made any attempt nor gave me the luxury of saying no. I still want to play the Christian. He would not allow me to touch him. He made sure that place was a *no go area*. I had some fears and began to think if this was real. But every time, he would say I should wait till the wedding day. Jesus said... the Bible says ... I never knew this was the dubious ways of Ibadan guys. *Ibadan guy, show me o!*

One day, my elder sister in Abuja asked me if we were sexually compatible. I said, 'the guy *no dey ask me for sex o'*. She said there could be danger in that.

Maybe he wants to trick me into marriage. My sister told me that the two of us must stand before each other and see *wetin we carry individually*. She said once our parents agreed that we could marry and they agreed to it, the wedding procedure was almost complete, and the rest was noise-making through the party.

After our introduction and engagement on a Wednesday, my husband was the first to disappear because I had told him he would *shine my congo* (make love to me) that night. He ran away. I went to his house; he was with his friends and would not come home. Uncle Bola, please do not think I am a pervert or desirous for sex. No. I just wanted to be sure I was doing the right thing. I have heard of so many men who tricked women into marriage, only to find that they were impotent.

I went to complain to the wife of my pastor. She said it was not right for me to be pushing him for sex. Since I know him as a Christian, maybe he was living up to that standard. At the risk of being seen as a sexual pervert, I held my peace. But my elder sister was always asking, have we '*shine our congo?*' (that was her language) I would say no, he is not even making any move. There were times we would sit together, and I would try to touch his penis stylishly, he would ward me off. I was like this born again *sha*!

We did our engagement on Wednesday and had the wedding on Thursday in Ibadan. I became wild with expectations. Right inside the car from the reception, I was trying to arouse him. I think this is normal. He was stiff. I was like, 'what now? Is this not the wedding day you have been talking about? We are moving right into the bedroom immediately we get home. Come and finish me, and I finish you'. He was not amused. I was like ...heee!

When we got home, he sat with his friends while I walked to the bedroom. He would not come in. I even heard his friends jokingly telling him to go and mark the *register*. What was he doing outside? I heard them. But he just sat there.

After a while, I called him on his phone that I was inside. He came in at about 8. pm. I was in bed, naked. He sat on the edge of the bed and started telling how great the reception was. I was just looking at him with fear and trepidation within me. After a while, he looked for my wrapper, covered himself, pulled off his trousers and put off the light, and wanted to climb on me. That was when I went wild. I stood up and shouted, 'No way. Today, I have to see *wetin* you *dey* hide in the last eight months. You got to see me, and I got to see you.' I told him point-blank that sex is not just climbing on me. There are procedures. Immediately I put on the light and took the wrapper from him, he lay on the bed, facing down. I told him I was ready to shout to everybody if he did not stand up and face me.

That was when he sat up. Come and see what he has for a penis! It is smaller than my last finger. It was barely visible. I broke down in tears. For a whole week, I did not speak to him. The pain within me till now is that he tricked me into marriage, and I fell for this because I was obeying the Scriptures that the bed must be undefiled and that our body, the temple of the living God. An Ibadan guy has duped me. Is this Christianity? Is this what I will face for the rest of my life? Why was I tricked into this marriage?

This is my second year in marriage. No sexual satisfaction. No conception till now. I do not even know where the problem is coming from. I know I can conceive because, in the past, I was once pregnant. Thank God for redemption. I do not ever feel him moving into me. It is like he is scratching my *congo*, supplementing that with his fingers. It is me constantly asking for sex. He will never make any move. And it is constantly climbing, climbing, and there he would be at the gate of my *congo*. I do not know how to tell it. I do not know how to go about this.

COUNSEL:

Please, do not blame yourself unnecessarily for not having premarital sex because this is a good and godly standard (Hebrews 13: 4). It is just a pity that your husband wasn't bold and honest enough with you to at least tell you his shortcoming before marriage. But you must be careful in your reaction also so as not to justify his fears in the first place. Remember, other young men with similar challenges may be reading this and would be tempted to conceal their conditions from their fiancées, assuming they would react the same way. Your case is not hopeless, though, as you can still conceive despite the small size of your husband's manhood. Penile enlargement is available also, but you will have to show your husband a lot of love and understanding to enlist his cooperation along this line. Be careful not to allow this challenge to pressure or lure you into extra-marital affairs, as that is a sin before God.

UNPROFITABLE RELATIONSHIP 14: MY HUSBAND IS FINANCIALLY UNCONTROLLABLE

She: Good morning sir, I have been one of your followers for now. I appreciate the grace of God upon your life, sir. May your source of wisdom never get dry! I have a problem I want you to share with the people of God to learn from their experiences. Can I share it, sir?

BOLA: Go on. Good morning my dear.

She: I am a married woman with two lovely kids. My husband is a pharmacist who earns at least a six-digit salary monthly. My problem is that he does not listen to me whenever I try to make him see reasons for having a budget and financial security. He has no savings. He spends money on ridiculous things and does not know how debt is being accumulated; huge debts at that. Sometimes we live well off, and other times, things would be so tight. I know I am not a wasteful or extravagant wife. I manage whatever he drops. Mind you, sir, we do not live together because of the nature of his work. He is in one state, while I am in another. Before mid-month, there is always nothing left to spend again. Please, sir, help me, I am getting tired of all this, I have prayed, yet no result.

BOLA: hmmm.

She: A family friend called and wanted me to try and talk to my husband to return their money. I was embarrassed. Sir, please, what can I do? His mum is also complaining of a lack of care every time. Please, help me. It is getting beyond control. I am still a nursing mother praying for a good job.

BOLA: Are you both Christians or Muslims?

She: I was from a Muslim background but now a Christian, and my hubby is from a Christian home.

BOLA: Does he go to Church? Do you?

She: Of course, sir – we are practising Christians. We attend RCCG together whenever he is around.

BOLA: Hmm... Let me pray for some minutes before I respond. I cannot speak now until I get direction and utterance from God. Please give me some minutes/hours. I hope you do not mind?

She: Alright. Thank you, Sir.

BOLA: Madam, do you care if I publish this matter on my wall without your name and profile, so we can hear what some people would say about it? Some friends could have opinions that could be useful, but If you do not want to listen to them, let me know.

She: No problem, sir, that's precisely part of what I want; to learn from you and others, sir.

COUNSEL:

It is a pity you and your husband are not

living together, and you are not presently working, though a nursing mother of two children. All that already paints a lousy picture financially! Please, make an effort for the two of you to come together in one place as soon as possible and get an excellent job to augment his income and watch out for improvement after a while. For now, your husband's six-figure salary is overstretched, flowing down too many drain pipes than it can cope with especially considering prevailing inflationary trends. While it is advisable to curtail your spiralling expenditures, you must expand your income base to stay afloat financially.

UNPROFITABLE RELATIONSHIP 15: REASON I CAN NOT HELP MY HUSBAND

I just read the post on why husbands are not comfortable with wives that are richer than them. I observed that so many people, especially men, say a lot of rubbish about women as if the men are not the source and origin of women's reaction, most of the time, if not all of the time.

I attended a women's prayer meeting at one of the Churches. A friend invited me there, and the Pastor preached on helpmate or something like that. He said God is placing women in prominent positions in life, and women have taken over the economic leadership in so many homes. But women have not been able to manage success, which is why so many homes are troubled. He said most women become arrogant immediately after being wealthier than their husbands. I do not think this is right. Pastors should not speak like that. They should not generalise. I do not think all women should be classified as the same. Let the men check themselves and find out why their wives would not help if they were more affluent.

So many women would not tell their husbands how much they earn because most men cannot stomach the successes of their wives. An example of such men is my husband and his father's house.

I got married to him almost 15 years ago. We had a blissful home until 2007, when things suddenly started happening. He lost his job at the bank and, since then, he has not been able to come back. It is like most people when they leave banking jobs, they have problems adjusting. My husband has not found his foot to date. I work at .... and my monthly salary and allowances are almost seven digits. I know I am ok. Thank God my husband is at home. He is not hungry. He has cars to drive, and I make sure I give him about 150k monthly. I am somewhat pleased with his condition because I have peace at home. My husband is not complaining, but his family and some people said that I should set him up in business. I do not know what their problems are if I cannot help my husband. How many of them can I tell this secret I want to share today so that some men who run their mouths would know that women, or rather, some of us, are not foolish?

My husband's family they are polygamous. All his brothers have two, three wives. All of them! He is the last child. Their stories are alike. They all have issues with their jobs, and it is their wives who put them back on their feet. Once they make it in life, they marry second wives, and the first wives are always sent out or abandoned—the women God used to make them.

I never knew this story until my husband lost his job, and we were naming our last child. The first wives, four of them, came at different times. They all told me the same story, how all their husbands lost their jobs, how the women helped them up and how they abandoned them. Same story! The same thing happened to my husband, and I am afraid the same may happen to me. Am I a fool? I do not want to be told 'we warned you'. Even their father was polygamous. Their grandfather too! All their uncles are. But I have promised God that it will not happen in my house. If my husband wants to, he is free to go and make his money, but I will not use my hand to do it myself.

As I said, I am not arrogant. My husband trusts me. He even said so to some of his friends that he has an obedient wife. And God sees my heart that I have never cheated on my husband ever since we married. And I will not. I keep a level and godly head. I love my husband, but the prospect of a particular second wife is scary. I am not holding my husband down. That Pastor should do his research on why women act the way they operate.

Uncle Bola, I believe I am in order.

COUNSEL:

You are not entirely in order in the sense that while it may be wrong for the Pastors or anyone to generalise about women, it is equally wrong for you to generalise about men. You are married only to one man and not all men in general. To every rule, there are always exceptions; there are exceptional men, just as there are amazing women in all aspects of life. However, you're in order so long as you assist your husband as much as possible and he is comfortable with that arrangement, and the two of you are happy.

UNPROFITABLE RELATIONSHIP 16: I WANT TO REMARRY, BUT MY TWO SONS SAY NO

I have wanted to discuss this matter with you for a long time, but I have been postponing it because I thought my children would have a change of heart, but they have not. It is like they are being selfish, thinking I should live my life for them all their lives. I cannot continue so, and that is why I am contacting you, and I want to hear from women like me who have gone through this same experience.

I am 44 years old. I had my first children, twins when I was just 19. We were seven children from our parents. Our father died when I was 15, leaving us for our mom, who was selling *akara*, beans cake, at the front of our house. I do not need to explain what we went through. You should know. The suffering knew no bounds.

There was a man who was always showing concern for us by giving my sisters and I money. We never knew he was an idiot. One day, I took *akara* to his house, and that was how he raped and deflowered me. This is a sad story in my life. I never knew I was pregnant, until one day when I told my mom that my menses had ceased. She said it must be *jedijedi.* I was given so many *agbo,* but nothing happened. She took me to the hospital, where she was told I was four months gone. The rest is history. To cut a long story short, the man came to our house to say he would marry me. He was 37. I was 18.

I put to bed and had twins when I was 19. My twins were barely one and a half years old when I was pregnant again. It was a baby girl, this time. She was hardly nine months old when I was pregnant again. A baby girl again! In four years, I had four children! It was a terrible experience for me. There was no husband and wife relationship between us, just sex, to cook his food, wash his clothes. Nothing more!

When I joined a Church in our neighbourhood, that was where some women who knew my story began to encourage me to return to school. When I told him, he said what are they doing in school and that he had no kobo to pay. The women's fellowship and partly my mom picked my bill all through. I did GCE, passed, and was admitted to Ibadan Polytechnic. Thank God education opened my eyes.

He would come to me in school that he wanted to have sex, so I should come home. When I told my friends in my room, he became a laughing stock. The children were with my mum. He would not give a penny for their upkeep. Sometimes the children would not see him for a whole month. If he went, he would buy *Okin* biscuits and give them a thousand naira.

When I started my HND, I stopped going to his house. I mean, I had no feeling for this bastard.

When I was to do my NYSC in Kaduna, I went to his house to pick my things and met him fighting with a woman. I later discovered she was his first wife in Ondo town, who had three grown children for him.

Since my NYSC, I have been living alone in Kaduna. My twins are now doing their master's degree and working in good places. They have steady relationships. My two girls are in universities. God has favoured me. This man is in Benin now. In the last 20 years, he came to see these children only twice in Ibadan. My children have no link to him because he did not even try to establish one. I must confess that I do not want to see him; I heard he had three other women after me. And that was what he was doing anywhere he was posted to work.

I have never had any serious relationship since I left this man. Men saw me as having too many responsibilities. They want to sleep with me and run. But God was faithful to me that I did not destroy myself. I have my dignity intact. I am a Deaconess in my Church, and I know that I am not fake.

I want to move on with my life. A man, legally divorced, came to propose to me that he does not need any children again. He has five already, and they are all graduates. He only needs a woman like me to be together. He came to my house those days, but my two boys drove him away. If he greeted them, they would not answer. Only my daughters understood and gave him attention.

I sat them down and explained that they would all leave me and set up their homes shortly. Would I be living alone? I told them that I was just 44, not an old woman. I need to live an entire life like a complete woman. They never responded. And they do not want to see any man with me, especially the boys.

There is another man I have known for two years now. He is a widower, a godly man just 47, three years older than me. For two years now, he has been there. He acts like a father to my girls. His three children are abroad. He was married to an American who died several years ago. He said he wants to move on but does not need a young lady because he needs no children again. But my boys are at it again.

The matter is getting bad between us now. I told them to get married fast and leave my house. I have my life to live. I have spent all my life on them. I put my life on hold all because of them. If I had remarried long ago, would they be where they all are today? Why would they not understand that I should live my life too? I am still looking good, and men still desire me. I am a top civil servant in this state. I want to live a happy life. My boys should let me be. This is my problem.

COUNSEL:

It is not a bad idea for you to remarry, but please, do not force it so you will not forfeit the love of the children you've laboured over

so much for years. Continue to pray and talk to them to persuade them and win them over to your side. You will always need their support later in life, even after re-marrying. And if I may suggest, the widower (from America) is far better than a thousand divorcees anywhere more so that you are a deaconess in your Church. But still, prayer and patience are the keys. I wish you the best!

UNPROFITABLE RELATIONSHIP 17:

INCEST IN THREE GENERATIONS!

I am 48 years old, a mother of four, 19, 17, 14, and 10, a boy and three girls. I have seen life at its best, and I am seeing the worst side now. I attend the Catholic Church. All my generations, dad and mom, are. I am an accountant and work with a construction company.

About five months ago, I never knew what woke me up in the middle of the night. My mind was fixed on my children, and I went straight to their room. The last child still sleeps in my room. Lo and behold, I found my first son right on top of his younger sister. I do not think I need to explain how I felt and what happened. I am a divorcee. They all live with me in a three-bedroom apartment. It was my saddest day. Not just because this happened, but because it also happened to me when I was 21. I was deflowered by my father's younger brother.

Deacon Bola, there was nobody I could discuss this matter with. I have never told anybody, living or dead, of this experience. No one! I just kept it to myself. But when I caught my children, I felt like dying. Until my mom, 68, approached me that I was looking sickly. I opened up to her about what happened to me over 24 years ago and what I saw my children doing.

My mom was silent for two days. She was withdrawn and began to fast. After a few days, she came to my house and opened up to me that she was also raped and deflowered by her father's younger brother, whom she stayed with when in teachers college in Zonkwa, Kaduna state. Uncle Bola, three generations!

My mom died in May from complications not far from high blood pressure. I do not know, but the last time I went for a medical check-up, I was told that my blood pressure was terrible. I do not know if this issue is the one disturbing me, or that my mother died in sadness. I have no one to open up to. This is not an issue to be discussed with anybody. Not even a reverend father. I want to hide under the anonymity of your wall for help.

I am aware you are a Pentecostal deacon, and Pentecostal Churches have understandings of issues like this. I have wept my eyes out. Now I want to grapple with the issue. What is responsible for this? My mom was a divorcee. I am a divorcee. I suffered rape and incest, my mom, too. When I sat down with my daughter, she confessed how it all started when she was about 15. Deacon, they have been doing it under my nose for years, and I never knew. How careless and too trusting of my children could I have been?

This matter makes me weep daily. My son left home since then, staying with his friend. I do not care to even check on him. I am deeply hurt. I have not been able to tell his dad. I do not even know if I should. My sorrows are many. My pains are many. Help me.

COUNSEL:

Your sudden discovery of incest in your family no doubt could be responsible for your raised blood pressure. It could be related to your mother's high blood pressure and death, since you discussed it with her and nothing was done about it before she passed on. Please, see a Pastor as soon as possible so he can take you and your children through deliverance prayer but be careful to ensure that the Pastor himself is genuine and does not end up abusing either you or your daughter in the process and complicate the matter. You will also need some counselling, especially in discussing the whole matter with your children and helping them relate better with each other and other people of the opposite sex.

UNPROFITABLE RELATIONSHIP 18:

DO NOT CREATE NEEDLESS PROBLEMS IN YOUR MARRIAGE

Please read the discussions below and see how some women create unnecessary marital problems. What you tolerate in courtship, do not complain about it in marriage.

SHE: I have been reading marital issues posted on your wall, but I have never shared mine because I believe I have a perfect marriage. However, I need your advice on this issue which has been bothering me since yesterday night that I saw it.

I was trying to send a message on WhatsApp, using my husband's phone, when I saw the profile of a female Church member. Reading through the notes, my husband commented on her beauty and dressing, and she replied, have you not seen the dress before? He even sent Valentine greetings to her. I was angry with him. It is unbelievable that my husband would pass comments on someone's dressing, looks, and eyebrows while he has never done the same to me since we married.

Even on our wedding day, he never mentioned how beautiful or ugly I was. During our courtship also, he never sent me any Valentine greetings. It has always been me doing the salutations. He finds it difficult to chat with me for a long time but takes pleasure in speaking with other people.

I am still wondering what could be going on between them because I have done all I could to make our marriage a perfect one. I obey every one of his rules. I do not make up either but because he likes ladies with makeup (not heavy ones, though), I decided to do it. I wonder what I might have done not to have ever received any praise from him even though I know he loves his child and I.

I do not know what to do because I have refused to share the bed with him since yesterday. I have also stopped talking with him. I am 30, and he is 32. Our marriage is two years now. Your advice is needed, sir. **Mrs. BIG**

BOLA: Hmmm, be careful! Stop looking for troubles where there is none. I know how painful it could be for women to find out that their husbands, who do not give them compliments, do so to other women. Men should know that women are super-sensitive in matters like this. However, you should try to overlook such issues when there is no evidence suggesting an affair between them. Just speak to your husband directly. If you can, tell him how it hurts to know that he knows the right thing to do, but he does not do it to you but other women. Open up, and do not be shy about it. He is your husband till death do you part.

SHE: Ok sir, but I said all this on Val's day and all he could say was 'sorry'.

BOLA: And do not push this matter too hard by not sleeping in bed or denying him sex.

SHE: I did that because he refused to say anything or respond to me. I was angry, cried and could not sleep all night. This morning I told him I could not continue with a relationship where I could not trust the man, so I want a divorce (lol).

BOLA: Hehehehehhe...lol. No! You have gone too far, but I think it is good to *shakara* your spouse once in a while, at least to show the depth of your hurt. I just hope he would know that *na shakara*, and he would be loving enough to make it up to you the best way he can.

SHE: I know he cannot bear to lose me, but I want to see his reactions.

BOLA: On Valentine's Day, if he failed to do it, why did you not? If he has never given you a present on Val's Day, why did you not try and do it, at least to show him the proper thing to do? I am sure if you do that, he will remember to be the first to do that next year. Husbands and wives must know that we must live a life of exchanging gifts.

SHE: I did because I know he will never say Happy Val, neither will he get me a gift. On my birthdays, there will be neither surprises nor gifts from him. I have been the one doing the giving all the time. I am just tired of his nonchalant attitude towards me when it comes to celebrations. Every of his birthday, I must get him a nice gift or a surprise party but in my case, nothing. On this Val's Day, I said Happy Valentine and even bought him a small gift I could afford.

BOLA: Now, let me ask a pertinent question: when you were courting, was he giving gifts? Doting all around you?

SHE: Nope.

BOLA: You mean he was not giving anything during courtship?

SHE: Once in a while and then, I believe, because he did not have much. He is not stingy o.

BOLA: Ok. Now... You have known his nature. It is not that he stopped doing it. He has been so all along. That is one thing about marriage. You knew that with him, and you did not complain then. You cannot change him now. Do not complain about what you tolerated. But you can speak about it once in a while. It is simply not his nature, after all, you said he is not stingy. So, it is not his nature. You tolerated him during courtship. Do not complain now. But mention it ... that you want him to show care, gifts and romance.

SHE: Ok.

BOLA: And know what, do not stop showing him care and giving gifts. And be prayerful. Tell God to touch him in that area. Men should understand the nature of women. Except women raised in hostile environments or have faced poor relationships all their lives, they love being appreciated. Let me tell you a story here: Last week, I went to see a very senior friend who gave me

N10, 000 MTN airtime. Already, I have about 5k airtime on my MTN line, so, I thought of selling the airtime. But I remembered the need to give my baby something. So, I decided to give all the N10, 000 airtime to her in N1000 every week. I started yesterday.

SHE: Nice one. Impressive!

BOLA: Now I realised that if I want to claim my title, baby could say *leg dey pain me, body dey pain me*. Of course, she gives in when I come but with some weak resistance like *na food*? *Sebi* you did one yesterday. I beg o, I am not getting younger o. *Ma so mi di apere Ajase o*. Such sentiments from wives when they are not ready for their husband's constant demands. Me, I am ready 247! Now since yesterday, I dey enter anyhow. Na my MTN card dey work.

SHE: Hahahahaha!

BOLA: Now, there are no body pains, no leg pains. Husbands should know how to catch their wives *mugu*. *Sebi na* your wife? Yoruba people say... *Ti enu ba je, oju a ti.* May God give us a great understanding and the ability to show appreciation to one another regularly in marriage! If we offer love and care, we would not be having problems all the time.

SHE: I am not a sex freak, but despite that, I do not deny him anytime he requests it.

BOLA: Even God, we should know how to catch God. He told us that with obedience, then with praise and worship, He would come down. Everybody has a price. Men should know the passwords that open their wives. God will touch your husband. Mention it to him. Show him also. Give him time. TIME! He will change.

SHE: Amen. Thank you so much, sir.

UNPROFITABLE RELATIONSHIP: 19

HOW CARELESS CAN SOME MEN BE!

Yesterday, minutes after I posted the issue from Mrs BIG who complained about her husband's nonchalant behaviour to her, another lady also chatted with me on the same issue. After my conversation with her, I concluded that indeed, some of us men have problems. Please read our discussion below.

I believe this would help some men see where and how they hurt their wives and inadvertently send love packing from their homes. Those things we see as unimportant and petty are exactly what God used to wire our women. They want their husbands to speak to them, observe them, comment on their dressings, give gifts, walk with them along the streets, identify with them, tell your friends about them, remember their important dates, celebrate them, love their children, call them during office hours, etc.

Guys, our wives want us to woo them from the first day we did to the end of their lives. Wooing them is a daily experience. Seriously if we do this, we would enjoy our

homes. I discovered this secret long ago. Whoever tells you that marriage is designed to be a battle is a LIAR. Find the password of your spouse, and you are in paradise. I do not think what the women want is unimportant. That is how God made them. It is not their fault. We need to sit up.

Please read.

SHE: Hello Bola, that conversation of the husband who does not appreciate his wife interests me. Mine is exactly like that, and it took me years to know that he loves me.

BOLA: Hmm.

SHE: No gift on Valentine's day, wedding anniversary, even birthday gift is by force.

BOLA: Hehehehehehe...lol (laughter)

SHE: So, I started by giving him. I got tired and stopped, made my conclusions, and moved on.

BOLA: Hmmm. Up till now, still the same?

SHE: He does not even know when I changed my hairdo. I might as well wear a yellow dress in the morning and return with green, he would not notice.

BOLA: Heheheheh...lol. Most men are like that. I guess we take our wives for granted. How come we remember these things when we were courting them? We treated them better during courtship.

SHE: But I get lots of compliments out there; in the office, everywhere. People comment, some foolish, though. A man even toasted me, asking me out on dates. Yet my husband does not notice me.

BOLA: I also think most married women do not express such observations either seriously or playfully. Women should make their feelings known. After all, men would react immediately if anything offends them.

SHE: But as we grow in the relationship, I realized that he is secretly proud of me, boasts about me to his friends, and somehow I got to know.

BOLA: Wow! Most men do that also. Should I say most or some or few...?

SHE: For me, the solution is to continue to look good, dress awesomely, make myself beautiful all the time. He still does not say it, but I know that he adores me.

BOLA: Great!

SHE: Gifts? He does not do that much, but I have also grown to ignore it. And when I am blessed I shower him with great gifts, not expecting anything from him. It takes time to get to that level, but that is the level of real joy in marriage; when you do things for your spouse without expecting anything in return. Today is 25 years after. We have had tough times. I did attempt to leave him once; he did not even ask me not to. So women should stop using divorce as a threat. It does not work! The man, even though loves you, will not bulge. If you continue with the threat, it may become real. It does not solve the problem. What we need to change our husbands is to change ourselves. When we change ourselves, we will wake up one day and discover that the man has changed.

BOLA: Hehehehehe...lol. Good one!

SHE: Do I like all he does? No! Does he cheat on me? I am not interested. I do not check his phones. I did that in the past and the only person that got hurt was me, not him. So, what am I looking for? He loves my children. He comes home to sleep. He eats my food and enjoys sex with me. We pray together. He is not God, so, he cannot supply all my needs. For the one he gives me, I am grateful. I miss him when he is not around and I share my daily stories with him. If all of this is love, then I love my husband.

COUNSEL:

I love your stand, madam, except for saying that you are not interested in knowing whether or not your husband cheats on you. God is interested! I am sure you want to be in heaven after your earthly life and would also love to see your husband there. Adultery is one major sin that could keep you out of heaven. So, please, be interested in that aspect of your marriage, if only for God's sake. Please, read Exodus 20: 14 and Hebrews 13: 4. God bless you.

UNPROFITABLE RELATIONSHIP: 20

I AM NOT COMFORTABLE WITH MY HUSBAND IN THIS CHURCH

We have been married for five years and blessed with a child. My husband told me before our wedding that he has believed God is calling him into ministry since his university days. After graduating from a university in the north, he moved to Lagos for the first time in his life. There, a friend took him to his Church, and he was accepted as a Pastor. The General Overseer (GO) is a middle-aged man who has some Pastors around him. He enrolled in a Bible school and was ordained there.

All this while, I lived in the North but sought a transfer to Lagos four years after he left. The first-day I got to this Church, I immediately perceived in my spirit that something was wrong here, and I told my husband. I picked it directly in my heart. My reading of the other Pastors is that they are all eye service people, some of them are retirees, some of them employed as Pastors, and everybody is here competing to please the GO for favours and promotions. The older Pastors there erect a kind of barricade around the GO. You cannot ordinarily see him. The Church is filled with artisans and market women. Few people are white-collar workers. It is a Church where you are told to bring water today, bring anointing oil tomorrow, bring a broom, bring a handkerchief, to fight the devil.

I keep my ear to the ground and hear that it is taboo for any pastor to do what the GO has not done or do what the GO is doing. If you do that, you would be seen as competing with him or you want to snatch Church members from him. Sincerely, we never heard this from the GO, but that consciousness is thick in the air.

My husband has the gift of writing, and he writes well under inspiration. But none of the eight older Pastors has written one book, even the two written by the GO were his sermons which some people translated into books. Please, I am not running down the GO, but I need to open up to you.

My husband has written four books, all still in manuscripts. He once told me that he briefly mentioned this at the Pastors' meeting and that he wants to publish them. After he said so, one of the older Pastors immediately cautioned him, *Erin ki fon ki omo e fon*, meaning he cannot shine while his seniors in the Church have not. I know the anointing my husband carries, and I felt so depressed. I told him we needed to move from this Church, but he refused, saying God had not told him so. What else does he want to hear from God that where we are is not the right place?

Another example: we have two cars, a Camry and an SUV. He couldn't dare drive the SUV to Church because they taunt him as a small boy acting like a big man. You often hear some of these old Pastors hail him *Baba Olowo* (the rich one), and I know what they mean. People come to tell us to be careful of this man, that man. Nobody trusts anybody. You hear that someone is a spy for the GO. Someone has *juju*. There is too much politics here. They suspect each other here. In a Church of God! I think my husband and I are too young for this experience. We have spent four years in the Church. They rarely give him roles on Sundays. He has never preached, only at Sunday school classes. He just sits somewhere behind. All his suggestions to put the Church online, even using his own money, is rebuffed.

My husband attended a Bible school and has a Master's degree. These people have a way of bringing down Bible schools. They say God's calling is not about Bible school. It is from them I hear that education is not important in ministry but the anointing. My husband is an engineer in a property company. He returns to Church every day after work. I am also a lecturer. He is 37. I was 34 in January.

It is not that I am impatient. I just feel he cannot grow here because of the negativity around him, yet he would not listen to me. We women see farther than you men, most times. Is my fear justified? Should I keep quiet? I see no future here. Uncle Bola, as a Pastor, what can a wife do? My spirit is not here.

Counsel:

I sincerely appreciate your concern for your husband. Your thoughts and fear for his ministerial life are indeed fair enough. Nonetheless, you must understand that "God's thoughts differ from our thoughts and His ways from our ways". Advising your husband to leave this church because of these present challenges is against God's will for him. It could be misleading and as well as affect his ministerial pursuit. What

is paramount at this time is, is your husband in the will of God? Is his present location God's destination for him? If the answers to these questions are yes, I will advise you to leave him alone to do what God has called him to do but continue supporting him. Put your mind to rest; all your worries and fears concerning your husband are stepping stones to build a better minister of him.

Finally, I will advise that you consistently pray for him that God will give him the wisdom to fulfill his ministerial calling in that church and if it is the will of God for him to leave, that the Lord should open his eyes and order his steps.

UNPROFITABLE RELATIONSHIP: 21

MY HUSBAND IS ADDICTED TO PORNOGRAPHY

Chatting with women, exchanging sex pictures, even in my presence

SHE: Greetings sir, I want to know if it is right to join my husband in watching porn films because he is addicted to it but still, our lovemaking is nothing to write home about, yet he claims he is not having extramarital affairs. He is fond of chatting online with all sorts of women from morning till night, and when I say he does not give me attention, his response is usually negative, telling me to go and look for someone to give me attention or someone to chat with. My question is, how far can a woman seek to know her husband? I find it difficult to believe or trust my husband because of the life he is living. I do not know the kind of friends he keeps. If I inquire, he would say what is my business.

BOLA: Give me more information: how did you meet him? Have you ever found him with any woman? Does he take care of you?

SHE: We met a long time ago when I was planning to travel. Twenty years later, he came, proposing as a widower with six children from five women. By that time, my marriage had failed 12 years before we met. After we started I discovered he was into several ladies via WhatsApp messages and phone calls, though none ever came around. But it was glaring he had other women and even after our wedding, he was still receiving calls from them sometimes late in the night, then I started reacting that it was not right. Most times, he would insult or abuse me even while chatting with the ladies. He would even say I am too jealous that, after all, he knew them before me, but when he prayed, he was told I am the best. So, why should I complain? There were times he would say if I want to leave the marriage, no problem. Later, when he calmed down, he would say he did not mean it. He only spoke out of anger, he could not do away with me. When I continued to show my aversion to this phone dating, he stopped the phone calls but chatting continued even when we are together on the bed. I dare not touch his phone except he asks me to. I cannot be free with him when he is on the phone. All these things give me much concern because such things cannot make a relationship trustworthy.

BOLA: I want you to give me comprehensive answers to these questions: What year did you meet him? Have you had any children for him since then? Are his six children in your home? Does he cater for them? Has he ever raised his hands against you? Why did you decide to marry a man with six children from five women? Were you not scared of his low level of responsibility and inability to be a good husband? Five women? You knew it and went into it, and you are now complaining? Talk to me ... Are you a Christian? Is he? What does your mind tell

you to do now?

SHE: I met him in 2012. I have a girl for him now. His kids are not living with us, they are with their respective mothers. He is not too close to them. He has never raised his hands against me. As for marrying him, honestly, based on what he said, in my mind, I thought he could be a changed person since there is no one without a past. It was later I realised the mess I got myself into. I got pregnant too early and we agreed to keep it. He said he had gone for prayers seriously because he too does not want his past mistake to repeat itself and since he had been told I am the only one to choose, so he did. I asked some pastors to pray for me too.

BOLA: ***On the pornography pictures, is he watching it alone or wants you to join him? At what point did it start with him? Have you discussed it with him and what did he say? You said your sexual relationship is bad. Is he weak or you refuse him sex***

always so he finds solace in pornography? Do you make efforts to know him very well before you decided to marry him? Do you find out why he has been so unsuccessful with all the women before you? How old is your marriage now? Do you give this marriage a chance?

SHE: On the pornography, he does not invite me to watch with him except sometimes he could just come up with it. He even exchanges with some women at times. On love-making, I am on the wounded side, he gives excuses for his poor performances. Severally when I discuss the pornographic habit with him, he would say he is just watching it, nothing more or shouts that I should leave him alone.

When I asked about the women, these were his answers: he got to know about the first child 20 years after birth because, according to him, he did not know the woman was pregnant. He was not allowed to marry the mother of the second child because of a misunderstanding between his grandparents and the lady's parents. The third lady left when they had a clash. The fourth lady, mother of three left him when, according to him, he fell into financial hardship. The fifth lady and the baby she was to have died during childbirth. It was three years after her death that we met and decided to marry. As I said, I did not take my time before we got married.

Though, he often ruefully says he made mistakes in the past which he did not pray for but still, he is the unstable type. He says a thing today and goes back to it. As for the porn films, it was along the line I discovered he watches it and he usually stays away with his phone so I may not know until I just bump on him. Our marriage is a year plus but I am not too comfortable with the way he does things. My mind is not settled. I do not know why. This issue of chatting with women, hiding his phone, lack of transparency, etc, give me concern. I am kind of developing a thick skin towards him though I am trying not to.

BOLA: Hmm. You have to be patient with him except you want out, and that will be your second failed marriage. In our society, you soon become an object of ridicule. We all have one life to live, therefore, keep yourself happy. Your happiness should not be dictated by anybody. The joy of the Lord should be your strength. So, whatever he does, keep yourself happy. It is in your hands. Overlook some issues. Find something to occupy your time with, believing that he would outgrow this habit someday. Where do you work? What business do you do?

SHE: Last year, I took a loan of N400, 000 just before the local government revoked my shop. Not to waste the money, I gave the loan to him and since then, nothing yet...

BOLA: You took a loan and handed it over

to him? And till now he has not given you back? How much

SHE: Well... I gave it to him to support his business. Is it not good?

BOLA: It is good. A good woman supports her husband, that is what the Bible says. But when giving such bits of help, you should be careful and be sure that it will not destroy your business. Men should struggle to set up their wives, to establish them, because when the crunch comes... men always fall back on their wives. For him to use the loan and not pay it back till now, such that your business is down, you applied no wisdom in this. Moreover, to a husband like this. But in all, you have acted as a good wife but he is not paying you back well. You are a good woman.

SHE: I am still worried about his habit of

exchanging porn films with ladies even besides me... he is fond of telling me if I go, he does not care, other ladies would take over. I do not know what sort of a man would say that and later say it was out of anger...

BOLA: I do not know how to cure a porn addict. Be patient. Avoid him as much as possible. This is one of the problems of marrying a man who has so many women in his life. He is never stable. It was an error for you to have been so careless to have settled for someone like that. Not at your age should you make such a mistake, not even with your experience. Come to think of it, you went ahead to have a child before you checked him out properly. You caused it. So be ready to face the music. And let me be sincere with you. He cannot change. It is too late for him to change. Except the Lord touches him or teaches him a lesson. No man can change another man but the Holy

Spirit! Please, enjoy yourself. So you either speak to the Holy Spirit or be determined to cope or ship out before becoming delirious.

Counsel:

First, you started your marital life with your husband on the wrong foot. You barely know him; I mean his personality before settling down with him. Your marital woes are the consequences of your mistake. I must inform you that your husband's addiction to pornography is an "emotional sickness." Your husband is sick, and this emotional sickness affects his sexual relationship with you. As long as the addiction continues, it will be difficult for him to satisfy you sexually.

If your child is sick, will you abandon him? I guess the answer is no. So, I believe that divorce is not the way out of your present predicament. The Bible says, "With men, it

is impossible, for with God all things are possible" Mark 10:27. As far as I know, what your husband is going through does not have a human or medical solution, but God can heal and deliver him and turn him around into a loving and caring husband. But that will be up to you. You must be ready to dedicatedly and fervently pray for his deliverance (healing), believing for a change in his life.

In the meantime, continue to love and be submissive to him; stop questioning his addiction. It is just a matter of time; he will come out clean, overcoming the addiction.

UNPROFITABLE RELATIONSHIP: 22

MUST I BECOME A PASTOR BECAUSE OF HIM?

I told him that if God has called him, God has not called me

I have an issue bothering me seriously. I am 29. He is 32. Our wedding is slated for December this year, but I need to clarify this issue before I run into problems.

He is a Pastor in a Pentecostal Church, and I worship in an Anglican Church in Ibadan. He has his eyes on starting his Church shortly. According to him, God has told him to move from the current Church where he has been a Pastor in the last eight years since he graduated. He prays well, speaks in tongue, anoints me with oil, gives me Holy Communion when I am sick, and people respect him in his Church despite his young age.

Now he said if he starts his Church, it is necessary for me, his wife, to also be Pastor Mrs. That I will be the one attending to women matters in the Church. He is forcing me to go to a Bible school and wants me to tag along with some women in his Church who go to Prayer Mountain all the time to pray. He said I should develop my prayer and fasting life. Here I am, I eat like a termite. Fasting is not my lifestyle. I am not a Pentecostal. I am an Anglican.

I love him, no doubt; he does too. But this religion matter is dividing us. I told him that if God has called him, God has not called me. It is not a must that every Pastor's wife must become a Pastor when God has not called her. He shows me the pictures of so many Pentecostal Pastors on posters and flyers, cuddling themselves with names like Bishop and Pastor Mrs He cited so many examples of Pastors and Pastor Mrs. I said I do not see myself becoming a Pastor because I fear God and will not go into what God has not called me to do. It is a thorny issue between us now.

While joking with him, I often hit him with some bitter truths, my observations of the Pentecostal churches. I told him that you Pentecostals always do things to suit yourselves, spend Church's money anyhow, subdue the Church under the pastor's whims and caprices, your pastor is your God, your all in all. No one can question your pastors or call him to order, you better leave the Church. Not so in our Anglican where we have order, tradition and history that no one can change except the Holy Spirit.

Now, I am 29 plus and this is the only relationship I am into in the last four years. It is like there are no husband materials out there again, only those who want to sleep with you and run away. I am afraid to leave him so I will not be alone. For that reason, I find myself speaking in tongues falsely and he seems happy. I will just be saying *prokokoko lelelele lamrama lamrama*.. But deep down in me I know I am lying.

Please, help me, must I build my marriage on falsehood? I am weeping as I am typing this. Where can I go now at almost 30? Must I dwell in falsehood? I am a graduate of UI. Last week, I followed the women to one Ori oke against my wish. I wept bitterly asking God why is this happening to me?

My question is, what can I do now? Is it true that once God calls husband, he also calls the wife? If God did not call me, can I call myself? Is it a must that if he becomes the GO of his Church, the Pentecostal tradition is that I must also become a pastor? I am a deep-rooted Anglican, my family is Anglican. He is a Pentecostal. Can this marriage work? At 30, will I still get a husband?

Tinuke.

Counsel:

Let us, first of all, address your falsehood in the area of speaking in other tongues. I will advise you to stop pretending, repent and ask God for forgiveness. Do not joke with spiritual things to please any man. Deception in courtship is a setup for a marital crisis. Be yourself. If your husband-to-be truly loves you, he will marry you for who you are and not try to change you into what you are not.

Be clear about your decision to marry him. Do you want to go ahead to marry him because you truly love him or because you are ageing and do not want to feel left behind? If you say you love him but do not like his pastoral calling and the Pentecostals, I will advise you to quit now and patiently wait for someone within the orthodox circle. But if you genuinely love each other and see a future in your union,

you both must be sincere and reach an agreement before saying, "I do." You do not have to be a Mummy G.O or Pastor Mrs., but certainly, you have a role in his life. Remember, if you marry him, you will become his helpmate.
Finally, I will advise that you both see a pastor or an elder or a marriage counsellor to further counsel you and broaden your understanding on this matter.

UNPROFITABLE RELATIONSHIP: 23

I DO NOT WANT TO BE GUILTY OF MURDER. WHAT CAN I DO NOW?

I am a 48-year-old married mother of four boys. My first child is 19 this year, and my last is nine years old. I am satisfied with the four boys, and I feel my husband is also comfortable. Initially, we planned to have two. But when the first and second turned out to be boys, we tried once more to have a baby girl, but it was a boy. We tried again, and it was a boy. So I crossed my leg. It is over with pregnancy.

But I always have problems with my husband. He does not use a condom. He said he wants skin to skin, and he feels he can withdraw in the nick of time. But he fails. This has led me to about eight pregnancies in the last six years, and each time, we have to go for Dilation and Curettage (D&C). At a stage, it became a big fight between us. I always say he wants to kill me. I do not want any more children, and yet he would not take precautions. I am the one suffering it. What bothers me most is the abortions which I do needlessly. I keep telling God that it is not my fault. What else can I do to a husband who will rape me at home, force me into sex anytime, and yet would not take precautions? I have reported this matter to my parents, and you know their usual counsel is to bear it. That is what women suffer in marriages.

The last time we did D&C, the doctor specifically warned my husband and I that no pregnancy must happen again except I want to die, adding that my womb is already infected. That day, I wept. Not until then that he start using condoms because I told him if I died over abortion, I would come back to kill him.

Now, I decided to contact you not because of this

but some new spiritual development. One day in 2016, I was speaking to the Pastor, husband of my friend, and he said that as he was praying that afternoon, he saw a baby girl running after me. I quickly shouted, 'I reject it.' At what age? No more children. We laughed over it, but his voice was a hint of seriousness.

Not long after that, I was on the express road to enter a bus when one woman accosted me. At first, I did not want to listen to her because I did not know her. But I changed my mind and gave her an audience. She said she is a prophetess, and as I passed by her, the spirit told her to look at me, and she saw a pretty baby girl running after me, asking me to carry her. Immediately I remembered what the Pastor said. I just left her standing there and went away.

In my office, all of us always pray together in the mornings before the commencement of work. There is a man who is like a Pastor or prophet in his Church. Late last year, one Monday morning, he said he saw me carrying a baby girl, who will inherit all my clothes and gold, etc., we all laughed over it.

Last month, my mother called me from home and said a white garment woman came to her street. While praying, she pointed towards her building that a woman is living in that building which is to give birth to a baby girl, and she is refusing, and the baby girl could kill the woman anytime from now because she has refused her entry into the world. Immediately my mum told me, I confessed the whole story to her, and the doctor warned me to steer clear of pregnancy. My mother said I should forget the doctor and take in, I should not kill myself. She began to weep. I do not believe in all these, but the continuity is starting to worry me.

I went to the doctor and told him the whole story. The doctor said I should forget all these religious people, they are after what they want to eat. If I try any pregnancy at my age and with the condition of my body, I will regret it. Now I am between the deep blue sea and the devil. This matter is worrying me sick. I am a Christian. I do not believe in these white garments, prophets, etc. but the matter is beginning to bother me. What evil baby girl is running after me at age 48? Why did she not come earlier?

I told my husband all of these, and he said I should forget it. He cannot start buying pampers at age 54. He thought I am the one making up the story because I want a baby girl. This matter is worrying me. I keep praying, but I do not want to be guilty of death either way. What can a Christian do now? Is this not the wiles of the devil? Where is this evil baby girl coming from, Uncle Bola?

Counsel:

I am happy that your husband has decided to put your health first by observing the sexual precautionary method. Concerning the prophecies on you giving birth to a baby girl coming from a white or coloured garment prophet (pastor) or prophetess, I

would say, do not throw caution to the wind. First, you are not young anymore, naturally above the age of menopause. Let me humbly say, there's nothing wrong with prophecies, but the bible says, "For as many as are led by the spirit of God, they are the (matured) sons of God" Romans 8:15

A prophecy is a confirmation of what is in your spirit. When you hear a warning and your heart (I do not mean your mind) disagrees with it, please discard it until you have peace inside of you and a conviction from the Spirit of God. Do not act on any prophecy regardless of the personality prophesying. Be patient, if this prophecy is from the Lord, He will reveal it to you or your husband.

UNPROFITABLE RELATIONSHIP: 24

HOW CAN I HANDLE MY HUSBAND'S FETISH WAYS?

I am 31 years old, my husband 36 and we have been married for six years but with no child yet. We have gone for several tests and found out that none of us has any issue and doctors said we should get just bond right and make love at the right time.

Also, my husband lost his job three years ago. The dry cleaning business he is doing has not been yielding much, but I am not bothered as his wife. I work in..... and earn well. I am covering up for him. I have never made him lack anything. I get him good clothes and put good food at home. Immediately I get my salary, I send N100, 000 into his account. I also know that when men find themselves in situations like this, they become extra-sensitive to how women talk. So, I am careful how I talk to him, lest he says I am rubbing it in.

However, my husband is not satisfied. He is a person who listens to so many people, pastors, prophets upon prophets who tell him that his problem is from his family. They even told him that I have a familiar spirit, that I am an *emere*, that I have *Ogbanje* spirit, that beautiful women like me must belong to their group. This matter has caused so much friction between us. I told him I am a child of God, and I do not have any familiar spirit anywhere.

At a stage, my husband started following his *woli* (prophet) friends to different prayer mountains. Sometimes, he would go for days and will not come back home. When he comes back, emaciated, hungry, dirty, he would say he was praying on the mountains, in the bush for children or better business. My husband has been so brainwashed by these *woli*. Sometimes before having sex with me, he would pray for a long time that I would have lost interest. He would anoint my breasts, private parts, dip his finger deep into me with oil, and anoint his penis and testicles, rubbing oil all over my buttocks.

All these things irritate me. Over what? That we want children? I told him I knew I would not be barren because that is not my covenant with God. I know what the Bible says concerning me. I stand by it and confess it daily. But my husband is in the wrong mix and is becoming fetish because his *woli* friends told him his problem is from his town or me, an *Ogbanje*. My husband travelled to his hometown to bring the sand in front of his father's compound, the sand on his father's grave, the water from a stream behind their compound and gave them to the *woli*.

He has over fifteen different bottles of anointing oil in our bedroom. He has different versions of the Bible in different shapes and sizes, same for wine for Holy Communion. He has over ten different kegs of water, water from river Jordan, the Atlantic Ocean and Osa Lagoon in Lagos, the stream in his village, etc. He has about four neck chains. Yesterday, he brought in pigeons which he said I should be feeding every morning. I asked him over what? Is he now a white garment Christian or still a Pentecostal Christian?

Deacon Bola, we attend a Pentecostal Church o. I am a member of ... and he was in one of these Pentecostals that we are not sure what they believe in. Should I not speak to my feet before my husband turns me to a fetish woman? I have reported the matter to my Pastor, who was at our wedding. He sent for him, but he would not go.

Anytime he is around, he watches the time to make love to me. 9am, 12noon, 3pm, 6pm, etc. He said those are the times angels are on duty. Now I have itching in my private part because of dipping oily fingers in me. I have spoken to him so many times in tears that he has gone astray but he will not listen. Should I comply with all his ways as a wife or find my level.

Counsel:

I applaud you for standing by your husband in maintaining peace in your home, especially in the area of finance. Concerning childbirth, your husband's behaviour is an attitude of the desperation of someone who wants a child at any cost. His desperation has led him far away from God, thereby indulging in fetish and occult practices that are harmful to your health. The bible says, "let your yes be yes, and your no be no". Nevertheless, you must be prayerful both for yourself and for the miracle of conceiving. The time has come for you to boldly (with love) refuse all of these shenanigans. Confront him and draw his attention to your health issues due to his unhealthy practices.

UNPROFITABLE RELATIONSHIP: 25

AN ESCAPE FROM A FETISH HUSBAND

After I posted the case of the lady whose husband is gradually becoming fetish, another lady chatted with me to discuss her experience and offer advice to the lady who wrote in—excerpts from the chats.

SHE: Good morning Uncle Bola. I just finished reading the post of the fetish husband and feel I should advise the woman here for security reasons. We both have similar experiences, but mine went on for six solid years until it became a nightmare for me. I reported to our Pastor on several occasions, but my husband would either refuse to honour his invitation or respond to him on the phone that I am just blowing things out of proportion. This went on for six years! Unfortunately, his parents are late, he does not have any respect or regard for his elders. The only woman he respects detested me with a great passion. So, I was in a fix of not knowing who to report him to in his family. And this man is a Deacon in our Church oooo.....hmmmm. It got to a point where he was taking my undies for prayers too, bringing all manner of concoctions to our home and even demanded we share separate bedrooms to enable him to pray properly.

His pursuits started affecting his sexual performances too, to the point that he could not last 60 seconds on me aside from the fact that sex became a nightmare for me. I was eventually diagnosed with first stage depression when it became unbearable for me and was even hospitalised at some point. It was after my discharge that I ran to my Dad for help. My dear father was so shocked that for 30 minutes, he was gazing at me without a word when he got to know it has been six years of this torment.

My dad sent for him, but he refused to show up for months. It was after that I decided to run for my dear life, and it has been three years now that we have been separated. I still suffered many afflictions for months as a result of the so many fetish items he was using on me. It got to a point that I started behaving like someone who was going insane or something. Uncle Bola, I cannot explain it all honestly, but my advice for that lady is that she should take a break in order not to break. If not for the mercies of God, I would have been history by now. I must submit to you that it is still affecting me to date because I have not been able to open myself up for any relationship because of fear of being used again. Please share if you wish. God bless you always for this forum.

BOLA: Wow! So you went through all this too? Na wah o. I praise God for your life.

SHE: Yes sir. Even more, than I can type here...

BOLA: I praise Him for delivering you.

SHE: Amen oooo

BOLA: You see, as a Christian, it is difficult for me to say the lady should get out of the marriage ...

SHE: That is why you should post my comment. It is better, please...

BOLA: God bless you for sharing your experience.

SHE: I am still shocked by this whole mess o

BOLA: And here you are looking pretty and good as if no wahala.

SHE: We did registry and I cannot remarry except I divorce officially. Thanks, sir. Lol. Na God o.

BOLA: So what do you want to do now?

SHE: Trying to process the divorce thing here but na money dey hold me.

BOLA: Hmm

SHE: A lawyer friend who wanted to assist me was almost taking advantage of me so I ran. Did I tell you he eventually used *magun* for me?

BOLA: Magun?

SHE: Yeah

BOLA: Is he a Yoruba man? Is he educated?

SHE: Thinking I was having an extramarital affair. So it started affecting me o. Yeah, he's a Yoruba man and educated too.

BOLA: And how did you survive the *magun* thing?

SHE: It was with the help of my father in the Lord (though late now). I spent almost N100k on it. I was almost running mad, I tell you. I will run temperature from a.m to p.m, and no medical problem could be discovered. That was when we had to start looking inwardly.

BOLA: Really? Looking inwards as how?

SHE: Some of my Pastor friends started fasting and praying for me, and were insisting it was an attack, though no one could place it until my daddy in the Lord who was based in Ikorodu, where I was staying before I got married, sent for me. According to him, while he was praying for me, he had a series of revelations about what the problem was. Meanwhile, I was seeing a lot of things too spiritually but felt it was my mindset and as a result of what I had gone through. Uncle Bola, look, *oro po ni we kobo...* (There is so much to say on this matter...)

UNPROFITABLE RELATIONSHIP: 26

WIFE MOURNING HER FIRST LOVE IN MY HOUSE!

Deacon Adewara, I woke up this morning with a feeling of profound sorrow and hurt in my mind because I just caught my wife in infidelity.

We have been married for three years. December last year, we were blessed with a child. When I met her, she told me some stories about her past even when I was not interested in knowing. I know my nature, I cannot stomach knowing men who have slept with my wife before me. She said in her Church, women are encouraged to confess their past lives to their husbands to be, blah blah blah. I only listened because she forced me to. That was how I got to know that she had dated four guys and slept with one, the person who deflowered her. She showed me the picture of her first love on Facebook and swore with the Bible that there is nothing between them again. I insisted she stop the Facebook friendship and she deleted him, but something tells me that my wife still secretly sees the guy. I have tried hard to catch her but to no avail.

On Monday, I found out that the man died in a motor accident. I saw his obituary on Instagram and Facebook but I kept quiet. What is my business? Though as a human, I sympathise with his family. I never knew how my wife got to know. She returned from work on Monday with red eyes. She was moody and was not her jovial self that night. At first, I never knew it was because the man died. I just felt she was just moody. From Monday till now Saturday, she is still the same and will not allow me sex. Yesterday morning, I asked her what is the problem. She just burst out weeping; telling me the man she told me about was dead. She fell on the chair weeping profusely. I just stood there looking at her.

Last night, I wanted to make love to her, and she said I should let her mourn her friend. I got angry and hit her. What an insult? This morning, I threw her loads out. I called her mother to come and take her away because I cannot stomach this insult any longer. The matter has gone so bad that I cannot even go to work today.

Deacon Adewara, I regard this as the height of an insult. A married woman weeping that her lover is dead! I need someone to discuss with because my head is hot. I cannot even think straight now. She has to go away from my house. I think this is a case of infidelity and the Bible permits me to divorce her.

Ola V.

Counsel:

You have a right to be angry at the moment, but I must say, your wife might probably

not be cheating on you, and this matter hasn't gotten to the point of suggesting divorce. There is absolutely nothing wrong with your wife mourning her friend (or ex-lover) but taking it to the extreme is what I frown at. Understandingly, women generally are emotionally fragile. Remember, the man in question used to be her lover, and over the years, they have maintained some friendship which she disclosed to you. It is natural of her to feel sorrowful and mourn such a friend but allowing it to affect your home and denying your sexual benevolence was wrong. Sir, two wrongs do not make a right. While your wife emotionally abused you, you, on the other hand, has violently abused her and also sent her packing. This case is easily resolvable. I warmly encourage you to swallow your pride, go to your mother-in-law and win the heart of your wife back. Ask for her forgiveness for hitting and

sending her out of her matrimonial home. I believe she will forgive you and ask for your forgiveness too for allowing her empathy for her ex overrides her matrimonial home obligations. God bless your union.

UNPROFITABLE RELATIONSHIP: 27

MISSING CLOTHES ANYTIME MY MOTHER-IN-LAW VISITS

I am newly married, got married two years ago to a lady from ... she is older than me, she is 33, and I am 31. I learned that she is older than me on our engagement day when a lady, my classmate at the university, saw her and said she is a friend to her eldest sister.

After the engagement, she came to my office and told me the whole story and I confronted my wife when I got home. Her response was, 'Did I ever ask her of her age, adding that all I was after was her figure 8 and sex. And, by the way, what has love got to do with age? Despite her age, is she not more beautiful and her breasts firmer and pointed than the younger girls I was dating before seeing her?

She was not repentant. She saw nothing wrong in withholding such vital information from me. I was to back out of the marriage but her mother intervened, rolling on the floor, weeping and begging that I should not bring shame to her family. Her mother reprimanded her severely that women shouldn't hide their ages and should be truthful at all times. Of course, I knew that the mother was in the knowledge of everything but just shedding crocodile tears when I am around.

My wife is not repentant at all. She is basking in the glory of her good looks. Deep down in me, something has changed. It has affected me. The wrinkles I did not see before, I am beginning to see them. I am seeing the bags below her eyelids. The African attitude of respecting older people is beginning to rear its head in me and ... I do not know really but I know I am negatively affected since I found out that I am married to my elder sister!

Her mother noticed this. She has called me twice to encourage me that age has nothing to do with love and when people even see us, I am looking much older than her and no one would suspect anything if I keep my mouth close. She said every family and marriage have their secrets. I have mine now, and I should show my wife that I love her. Anyway, I did not report the matter to my family or anybody. You are the first I am opening up to in two, three years now.

Now, since the wedding day that the mother left my house, I have been noticing something strange. My property, especially my clothes like shorts, trousers, shoes, chains, boxers, always miss. It was much later I discovered that a few days after she left, something of mine will be missing. I have been noticing this, but I could not summon the courage to confront my wife or else she would ask whether I am calling her mother a thief and what would she do with my things.

There was a day the mother came with soup of fish, snail, bush meat, etc and said all of us should eat together. Her body language held so much suspicion and I declined, saying I was full now and would eat later, and I left them. The mother would come in unannounced. She would say she came to rest in our place. We live in a three-bedroom apartment and she has taken a room for herself. She would even lock it and go with the keys. Anytime she comes, she comes with bills for me to pay. Clothes for parties, *gele* (head tie), her friend is sick she wants me to help the friend with hospital bills—all sorts.

I am into the Property market, and God has blessed me so much within a short time. I have three vehicles, including an SUV and we are living in my building. The mother keeps asking me to buy her a car and I have promised to get her a CRV. The mother lives alone. No husband. She has five children for three men. I discovered all these after our wedding. My wife never for one day told me anything like this. Two years into marriage, she has not conceived. I am even tired of sex with her.

Uncle Bola, my pain is I do not have anybody intimate to report this matter to. My mother died in a motor accident in January last year and I have only one younger brother in the university whose bill I am picking. Our dad remarried five months after our mother's death to a woman who does not love us. So, we steer clear of them. There are so many things I would have loved to discuss with my mother, but she is dead. This is the time I feel her absence most. I need a confidant. Someone I can open up to, who can be there for me. How can I resolve this area of my life?

The mother came Friday last week and left Monday. I just discovered this morning, Wednesday that my sandals are missing. What could be wrong?

Counsel:

Discovering that your wife is older than you isn't a big deal. I am sure there are virtues

(qualities) your saw in her that made you overlook the subject of age in your conversation with her during your courtship. **She is your wife and not your elder sister and she will never be. You are allowing your knowledge of your age difference to affect your relationship with your wife. According to you, you look older than her in appearance, and no one would suspect anything if you keep your mouth close. So, what is the big deal? My brother, do not play the blame game; it will lead you nowhere. Love your wife and enjoy what you have. All that matters is your love, trust and understanding of each other. Concerning the items anytime your mother-in-law is around, my counsel is this: speak sincerely with your wife about your observations. You never know if she, too, has been noticing strange things as well. Your findings will help you on the next step to take.**

UNPROFITABLE RELATIONSHIP: 28

HOW DO YOU ASK FOR FORGIVENESS FROM A WOMAN YOU HURT?

Martha, mother of four girls, is an object of ridicule amongst her in-laws on account of the sex of her children. Even some of her friends do mock her once in a while. How many people are literate enough to know that the man determines the sex of a child? Yet the illiterate society places the blame on women.

The search for a male child led Martha from one Church to the other. It was with trepidation she had the fifth pregnancy. She must have a boy at all cost to guarantee her marriage. That is the level some women descend to. When she put to bed the fifth time, it was a girl again. It was a big shame! She wept bitterly in the hospital. She could not send a message to her Church. She just stayed away, resolving that her Pastor has no genuine calling.

After about three weeks of disappearance, the Church sent a delegation to check on her. They heard her story of pains and mockery on account of five girls. They spoke and prayed with her, and she agreed to come back. As she was stepping into the Church on Sunday, a familiar Usher greeted her as he carried the baby. Noticing that the baby is a girl, the Usher shouted '*Haaa! Na girl you born again? You no go kill your husband with girls. Only you, five girls! Una go buy sanitary pads taya*." The Usher laughed extravagantly.

It was too much for her. Martha broke down in tears. Weeping loudly as she collected her baby and began to walk out of the Church. The Usher started to apologise that he was just joking, after all, they joke together always. Martha would not hear of that.

"I have been subjected to enough mockery in my family. People call me Mama Abi girls (Abigail). My in-laws are threatening my marriage, that my husband would soon marry the second wife because he is a prince who must have a male child. I came to God to help me. And still, I have a girl. Now, someone in the Church is mocking me again. Ah! Na so life be? OK o. I am going home."

More ushers surrounded her, apologising and explaining the offending Usher was only joking. It took them a long time to settle with her. To date, Martha is not on speaking terms with the Usher. She would not just wait to speak with him. At a stage, she shouted at him to leave her alone.

When the usher showed her to me yesterday, I resolved to go speak with her today, Saturday. But I do not want to be insulted by any hurting women. How do you speak to women in such a state of mind? Any suggestion?

Counsel:

First, the attitude of the usher was very immature. This is why church leaders must educate and train their congregation, especially the Church workforce, on human relations. Joking with such a sensitive matter was carnal of the usher. My question is, where is her husband in all of these? It does not matter who is mocking her from her in-laws' corner or joking with her situation in the church. What matters is the stand of her husband. Secondly, women should understand that biologically, they do not determine the gender of a child. Please, see a doctor for a further medical explanation. Nevertheless,

be strong in the Lord. Encourage yourself; be happy with what you have. Do not allow any external forces to rob you of your joy. Forgive your in-laws and the mocking (joking) usher. If it pleases you and your husband to conceive again, trust in the Lord, for with God all things are possible, and I assure you by the spirit of God, He will bless your womb, and you shall bring forth your Isaac.

UNPROFITABLE RELATIONSHIP: 29

HOW CAN I RESPOND TO DADDY, MY SISTER'S HUSBAND?

I decided to contact you now because I want to move out of this house in this New Year. I currently live with my elder sister, our firstborn. She is 48, a health worker, religious, a mother of two and always in the hospital. Her husband is 54. He loves life, a club man who drinks... with his big tummy. We respect him so much in our family because he acts like our father. We call him daddy. He sent us money when I was in university and to my siblings, who are still schooling.

My problem is with him. Ever since I came to live with them after my NYSC in Kastina Ala in Benue State, my ordeal started. While discussing and sitting close to him in the living room, he would touch me on my shoulders, laps, tummy as if stressing a point, even right in the presence of my sister. So, we had no suspicion, not until one day that he came back from work and I tried to hug him as usual, and his hand was right on my breast. I thought it was a mistake, but when he began to stroke me, I moved back and went inside my room.

He came to me and said take, stretching his hands to me. I rose from the bed, I did not know what to do. I could not refuse it either. We called him daddy, and he was kind to us. I took the money. He said, 'buy yourself something' and he walked out. When I counted the money, it was N50, 000. Since then, he keeps giving me money all the time, most especially in the absence of my sister. Why now in the absence of my sister? But since then, I have been on my guard, very watchful and sensitive to his moves.

Early last year, I got a job. He got the job for me. One day he called me in the afternoon to have lunch with him. I told him I was busy, but he still came. I could not be rude or shun him. I still have some regard for him despite his moves. He took me to his clubhouse where he was posing with me as his babe. After we ate all sorts, he led me to a room. I was unsure if to enter or not. I was so confused but walked in almost reluctantly. I stood still by the wall, refusing to sit on the bed. There was no chair in the room. He sat on the bed and began to undress to his boxers. I began to wonder: is this how I will sleep with my sister's husband? I braced up the courage and walked out, back to my office.

At home that evening, it was like nothing had happened. He was his jovial self, came home with gifts for all of us. My sister seems happy with him, ignorant of his misbehaviour. I was also cheerful with him but occasionally looked at him with bad eyes when our eyes meet. I kept wondering how my sister does not know that her husband is a serpent?

Not long after this, the daughter of my sister's friend came to spend a holiday with us. Before long, I noticed a romantic move between them when he could not get me. One day, I overheard their discussions, and my street sense told me *something dey shele*. I am a sensitive person. But my sister's Church attitude has blinded her. If I know that girl very well, I know daddy must have slept with her. She is loose and money conscious.

I feel like telling my sister. So, I discussed the issue in my office with some elderly ladies without saying it happened to me. I said it is my friend. The elderly ladies said that my friend would regret opening her mouth, especially if her sister trusts her husband. Her sister would say she is the one seducing her husband. They said she should let her sister discover her husband herself. She should find her way out of the house.

Uncle Bola, is this advice sound? How my sister has not discovered who her husband is till now bothers me. Or could she be pretending and expose us to this risk? I feel I need to warn her. She means so much to us. She takes care of us. Also, if I move out of the house, will he not be disturbing me wherever I am? Why are men this shameless? For crying out loud, why me, your wife's sister? Why me?

Counsel:

You have done very well in resisting all sexual advances and temptations to compromise your moral stand from your brother-in-law (daddy). Many ladies would have given in not minding the consequences.

My advice to you is this, do not be the one to let the cat out of the bag. It might backfire. Since you mentioned that your sister is a religious person, I suggest you approach her pastor and share your experiences and

shreds of evidence with him. Matters like this are very sensitive and requires a lot of caution. I firmly believe the pastor, by the grace and wisdom of God, knows how to counsel your sister and handle whatever be the outcome. As for you, please move out of the house. It is time for you to move on with your life.

Lastly, do not go out on any date or lunchtime or follow him to his clubhouse ever again. You may not have it easy like the last time.

UNPROFITABLE RELATIONSHIP: 30

WHAT IS THE LIMIT OF TRUST IN MARRIAGE?

The challenges some women face in their matrimonial homes are not just about unpaid dowries, the fruit of the womb, etc. So many women are so careless in marriages. I do not know if love makes women stupid or stops them from asking relevant questions or knowing the truth in their love dealings with their husbands. So many women do not know some fundamental facts about their husbands: the schools they attended, where they work or claimed to have worked if they have children before getting married, etc.

A lady, who had an issue with her husband, recently told me she does not know which university he attended, adding that she only su/spected he must be a graduate though unemployed when they met and got married. After all, love is blind. A few years into marriage, the lady picking the bills got tired. The eyes of love that were blind popped open. The lady asked him to get a job. She began to tell people that her husband needs a job. The people she met told her to bring his CV and papers. That was when the problem began. After three months of waiting for his papers, she confronted him and later found out that the guy was a loafer who dresses well. He did not go beyond secondary school and was not doing anything other than basking in the vainglory of his family's wealth. After enduring for a few months, the marriage crumbled. The lady's parents came to pack her loads from the house.

You can blame the lady, but have you checked yourself? Are you sure if you are asked ten questions about your husband, you will have the right answers?

Early last year, a woman lost her husband. Some three months ago, a lady came from nowhere to claim ownership of the second house left behind by the man. It is a six flat rented out. The lady went to the tenants and told them she is now the rightful owner of the building. She gave all the tenants photocopies of the CofO, plans, various papers with which the land was bought in the name of the late man and her name. This is the latest story I am treating now. Immediately I post this story, I will be on my way to Sango to meet the lady. She needs my help on how to fight back and claim ownership of the house. But I guess the battle is lost already.

Her late husband had another woman's name on all the papers. She showed me the photocopies she got from the tenants. They have gone to Ogun state where the CofO was done. The papers are original, not forged. She was married to him for 15 years. They both bought the land not far from Winners Church and built the house together. She said she sold two plots of land in Ikorodu which she inherited from her father's estate after his death, to commence the development of that building. She had never asked her husband for the papers. She believed him. She was in love. And she is not aware her husband had any wife or children anywhere. The man died last year. The property has gone to another woman.

The man had another wife out there and the woman never knew. Love is blind, right? Yes, love should be blind. You should love without limits, but that does not stop you from carrying out the necessary checks once in a while. The Russians have a saying: *doveryay, no proveryay.* In English, it means 'Trust but verify'. You can trust people but do not still forget to verify issues. Why? Man will always be man.

The same story can happen to you. do not ever say I trust my husband, it will never happen to me. Today, ask him for the papers of the property you own together. The property should not bear Mr. and Mrs. Bola Adewara, featuring just the husband's name. Any woman can be the Mrs. Adewara. It should therefore bear your both names, if possible, put your *oriki*. Mr. Bola Olusegun Adewara and Mrs. Toun Adunni Adewara. If possible put Nee Adekanmbi.

The question is this: is there no limit to trust in marriage?

Counsel:

You see, many of these failed marriages are the result of fouled courtship. Many of these courtships are "mirage based", that is, built around going to eateries on a regular date, romantic talk, and sex. They never discuss real-life issues relating to their personalities. So the lady never gets to know her man's true identity and vice versa.

Also, when coming into marriage, it seems the only subject in the mind of the intending

couple is 'love' and true is the saying, love is blind. Let me tell you, for any marriage to work or be successful, it must be built on 'love and trust'. If your husband-to-be cannot be trusted with money or he goes around with anything in a skirt and keeps coming back to you asking for forgiveness, take it from me, quit that relationship. If you get married to such a person, one day he will grow a thick skin in covering up his evil vices. And this is the case with many ladies.

Our fathers (and mothers) never had this kind of issues, because love and trust was the strength of their marriage life. I think it is high time we went back on time and learn from them, for these are the core values of the scripture on marital issues.

UNPROFITABLE RELATIONSHIP: 31

AT WHAT POINT CAN YOU START SLEEPING WITH YOUR WOMAN?

Your articles on the social media have assisted me in my choice of spouse. I finally picked a woman as a wife and we did our family introduction recently. I am determined to keep the bed undefiled. I have not touched her breast till now, how much more sleep with her.

But my fiancée is not taking things easy with me. She said her elder sister fell into the wrong hand five years ago when the guy she married also insisted on keeping the bed undefiled and he ended up with a low sperm count and half erection. Five years now, no conception, no enjoyment of sex. All they do is spending on different herbs and parading different hospitals.

My fiancée said her mother's friends told her to be suspicious of men or women who want to hide behind religion to deceive people into marriage, adding that devastated by her elder sister's experience, her mother insists she has to test me very well before the wedding. I told her it is a sin. She said there is no sin God will not forgive, moreover, we have done introduction, we are both known to our parents and our families now know each other.

Now that we have done our introduction and wedding is slated for February next year, she is insisting we can make love and she wants to be pregnant before the wedding. It is her candid view that once the introduction is done and both parents accented to our union, marriage is done, the rest is ceremony.

I am 28 plus from Abeokuta, based in Lagos. She is almost 30, a year and half older than me, from Benin also based in Lagos. Hardly would anybody know they are not Yoruba proper because their surname is Yoruba, all the children bear Yoruba names and they all speak Yoruba language fluently. We both work in a bank but in different branches. My Pastor knows her, and her priest knows me. I attend a Pentecostal Church, she is Catholic.

My question: is wedding done after the introduction? Can I start sleeping with her now? I hope I will not offend God if I do. Please respond to me. I also like to read the comments of your friends.

KaBiTi.

Counsel:

An introduction is not the same as a wedding, neither is it a license to have sexual intercourse with your wife-to-be. If you do, it is fornication and a great sin before God. 1 Corinthians 7: 1-2. I will encourage you not to be crossed with your partner, her motive and actions are sincere resulting from her sister's experience and as well many ladies are caught in the web of such predicament after the wedding. And she's not ready to be another victim of such.

Nevertheless, if you, on the other hand, is sincere in keeping the bed undefiled in obedience to the word of God and have no skeleton in your cupboard, I will suggest that you both go to the hospital of her

choice for you to have a genital test to confirm to her that you are sexually fit and capable of impregnating a woman. This will help in clearing her doubt and relieving you of any pressure to indulge in pre-marital affair.

UNPROFITABLE RELATIONSHIP: 32

HOW GOD DEALT WITH ME OVER UNPAID BRIDE PRICE

Your earlier posts on trust in marriage, when should a man start sleeping with his wife, etc, really touched me. I copied them, printed them out and shared them among my children, biological and spiritual.

Lest I forget, I am a preacher and general overseer of a Church. Kindly edit out some of my details. You can share my experience, not my person. I want to tell you my story, how I got married to my wife and have seven children without paying her bride price and how God dealt with me over it.

When I was 23, a teacher in a secondary school, I went to spend a Christmas holiday with my friends in one of the villages in Oyo state. My friends introduced a lady to me to spend Christmas with. They said she was my Christmas gift and that I should know how to manage her so that she would not be pregnant for me. But I made a big mistake. Every day, this village girl would bring breakfast, lunch and supper and anytime she brought the food, I would sleep with her. This village girl had a way of preparing food, especially, *eba and egusi* soup. Oh my God! Unknown to me, she had her plans. She was telling everybody that she is my wife but to me, I was just *rocking* her as a Christmas gift.

I was in school around February in the early1980 when my friend was led by police to my school. Behind him were the village girl and three women. She was pregnant and my friend was claiming not to know where I was until it became a police case. Some months later, she put to bed a set of twins, two girls. That was how the problem started. I was not a Christian then, did not even go to Church. It was a sorrowful experience.

Anyway, that was how I became a father and husband. She was brought to my house at Ijebu Ode and we began to live as a couple. And know what, everything was still like a joke to me. I never understood the implication of what I was doing.

Less than a year later, she became pregnant again. Her family began to insist I come to pay her bride price and organise the wedding. I refused. I arrogantly spoke to them to come and pick their illiterate daughter. Deep down in me, I was not ready to marry her. She did not know my family, nor did my parents know that I was already a father of three. All they knew I was doing then was beer, cigarettes and women. Not until the third pregnancy, the fourth child that my dad and mom came to Ijebu Ode in a surprise visit. They said they heard that I was married and hid my family from them. That was when I explained how it all happened.

Even until that time, I insisted I would not marry her because she was just a school certificate holder. I was already doing my degree course at the University of Ibadan. Her dressing was below the standard I wanted. Her spoken English was merely passable. In fact, I was not proud of her. I was just sleeping with her because she made 'it' available.

Five, six years after meeting her, she has had four children for me. It was like she wanted to punish me. Anytime I slept with her, she would be pregnant. I became helpless in 1992 when she had the second set of twins making six children. The first set was girls, the second set, girls. I now have four girls and two boys, from a woman whose bride price was not paid, a woman I could not say I love.

PART TWO

By 1993, a year after my second set of twins were born, the urge to give my life to Christ began after listening to a sermon by Billy Graham. I had dropped drinking and smoking habits long before then and was living a responsible life. I had joined a Church in Lagos and lecturing in a tertiary institution. The incessant fights between my wife and I had stopped. My children were having the best of education, and God had blessed me materially and financially. My wife, too, had started a course in a polytechnic, and she was looking up.

My decision to give my life to Christ and work for him was more of determination to show gratitude to God. My instinct sent me to the seminary and three years after graduating, I was sent to a new Parish which flourished well. But I know that I had a challenge somewhere. I had not paid the bride price of my wife. Anytime my Church members invite me to their engagements, I feel reluctant to go because I had not honoured my commitment to my wife. It became a big secret challenge for me. Let me tell you that all of us Pastors, have our challenges. No Pastor is free.

PART THREE

Fast forward to 2005: my first set of twins, now 23 years old, came to tell me that they want to get married in some months. That was where my problem started. For about five days, I saw a man in white, so furious, telling me that I was joking with my ministry, adding that I wanted to take the bride price on my children when I had not paid that of my wife. The last dream I had on this was when the same old man said if I receive that bride price, I will die a few days after. That was the last dream, and the dream stopped.

Immediately, I had the last dream, I woke and began to pray, asking God for forgiveness. That day, I went to see my father in the Lord and told him the story of my life. Angrily, he rebuked me and said, right now I should invite my wife to join us where we were. She came, and he confronted her.

She narrated how we met and how I had refused to pay her bride price or even do a proper wedding for her. She said she had been asking God prayerfully, wondering whether she would not wear the white gown ladies wear. She narrated how her father died unhappy that the bride price of his first daughter was not paid, claiming one man denied him his right over his first daughter. She said there was a day her father made an angry statement that the day her husband would receive the bride price on his twin daughters, he would drop dead. That was how the dream became clear to me and my father in the Lord.

My wife has been an obedient woman. I wonder if I was married to another woman, I would attain my status today. I have no problem whatsoever with her. Upon all, she gave me two sets of twins and other brilliant children I am so proud of. My wife said I made her look so cheap before her family such that none of them respects her, and that they were waiting for me to make amends.

My father in the Lord now said it was a must that I visit the family of my wife afresh, pay the bride price and do the kind of wedding she had always wanted before my daughters could get married. My wife was told to contact her family for the engagement requirements. That was where another crisis of exploitation began. They asked for the impossible!

PART FIVE

Deacon Bola, this is the list they sent in 2005.

1. Jeep 2005 model
2. 100 tubers of yam
3. 10 jerry cans of 25 litres of palm oil
4. 10 jerry cans of 25 litres of groundnut oil

5. 20 bunches of unripe plantain with the stalk
6. 200 pieces of orange
7. 100 pieces of unripe pineapple
8. 10 pregnant goats
7. Five baskets of tomatoes
8. Five baskets of pepper
9. Five baskets of smoked fish
10. Five baskets of bushmeat
11. 10 boxes full of new lace material
12. 10 boxes full of shoes
13. A jewellery box full of gold earrings and necklaces
14. Four return tickets to Jerusalem
15. 300 loaves of bread

Counsel:

I bless the Lord for your life, especially your sincerity in your story. You have proven that you are a nobleman of God who seeks to please his Master. You see, the above dowry list is proof that your wife's family are still very much angry with you. I do not think they are trying to exploit you but rather expressing their grievances. Asking

your wife to contact her family for the dowry list is wrong on your part and an insult to the family. Though your motive may be right, your action is a demonstration of pride, and so the dowry list was sent to humble you.

I humbly advise that both you, your family and if your father in the Lord is available, should travel down to see your wife's family.

First, to seek their forgiveness for your past mistakes.

Secondly, to properly ask for the dowry list; negotiate and reach an agreement and finally, fix a date for the wedding.

God's guidance and wisdom will surely see you through.

UNPROFITABLE RELATIONSHIP: 33

HOW DO I OVERCOME THIS ATTITUDE?

My husband and I love each other so much. I can go to any length to do things just to please him, same with me. We are like best of friends, but there's this attitude of his I do not like. I have done all I could to change him in the last six years, and he is not changing. It often leads to issues between us.

He says I complain and nag a lot, but the only thing I complain and nag about has to do with his weaknesses: he scatters the house a lot, He does not keep things in order and I hate dirty environments. I do not know why, when things are not where they should be, it has a way of irritating me. I am like a perfectionist. That was how I was trained and it is too late to change me now.

My husband will come from work drop his shoes,

stockings anywhere. In the bathroom, he would leave his boxers. You can find his slippers in the kitchen. He would use his toothbrush today and be looking for it the following morning. Later, we find the brush on the generator outside, maybe he went there to change the switch when NEPA takes light. My husband will use everything and will never participate in putting the home in order. He has never washed the plates before nor tried to show compassion that it is only me doing all this work. I close from work, rush home, cook food, wash plates, put the house in order, scrub the floor, lay the bed, wash the toilets, I mean, I keep the house in good order. I would be dead tired... and when I go to bed to rest, he is there again, *Folake, ki lon happen?* When I say 'no, I am tired', trouble starts and that is when I talk anyhow...

You men do not know how difficult it is for us women to be running from pillar to post to take care of the house and the next minute a man is scattering it. All our three children are in boarding houses. I can notice the two boys are taking after him gradually. They are just careless and carefree like him. Buy anything for them when going to school, they will not bring it back home on holidays. We have to buy new ones. As I am typing this, one of my husband's boxers is under the table. What is his boxer doing here? So, I complain about this and I get really angry and I talk.., but believe me, even after complaining, I regret my actions. I tell myself, you shouldn't have talked to him that way, he's your husband.

Before I got married, I desired to be a very good wife to my husband, even if he decides to be bad, but in this aspect, I have failed woefully. Apart from this issue, he does not complain about any other thing about me. I have prayed so many times, for the grace to tolerate it, not just tolerating it, but tolerating it with joy and overlook, but each time he repeats it, I find myself complaining again. Please how do I overcome this attitude of mine?

FLK.

Counsel:

The attitude of your husband is not strange. Some men (and women) are just weird like that. I love the fact that you honestly want to stop this attitude of nagging at him whenever he carelessly does these things, and you have prayed about it. The Bible says, "Faith without work is dead" James 2:20. For you to overcome this attitude of nagging, you must consciously work at it. Your willingness to tolerate your husband must not just be from your head but your heart.

I cannot guarantee that your husband will change in this area, and if he will, it will not be overnight. But with patience and good conduct, you will be able to tolerate him. And he, on the other hand, will always appreciate your gestures, and sooner or later, he will consciously begin to adjust.

Moreover, the devil knows how to keep you tormented in this area because you get hurt by this action. Make up your mind to have joy notwithstanding, even when picking up the things he throws about. I am assuring you it will soon end when the devil sees that it is no more hurting you.

UNPROFITABLE RELATIONSHIP: 34

DECEIVED INTO MARRIAGE BY A BIBLE CARRYING LOAFER

Now, after four children, what can I do?

My marriage will be ten years old shortly, and I have lived unhappily for about nine of those years. I live in constant anger, bitterness and deep frustration. Only my four children are my consolation, and I do not know how long I can go on like this.

I met my husband at the wedding of a family friend. He did not come to me directly, he spoke to the groom who talked to my elder sister, and she introduced him to me. From the day we met, I told him I wasn't interested in a casual relationship or sleeping around. He said he was not playing around either because he wanted to settle down. Whenever he came visiting, he was with his Bible, either coming from or going to Church. Any time we chatted on the phone, you find him quoting verses of the Bible. Every morning, he would send me on Whatsapp all manners of devotional, Christian videos, Biblical messages, etc. When I eventually visited him, I saw that he had a few pieces of furniture but plenty of Christian books and tapes. All these made me happy that I have met a God-fearing man with whom I can build a future. In all our discussions, he had big dreams and purposes.

Immediately after our wedding, things started changing rapidly: two weeks after the wedding, a lady kept coming to look for him with an angry face, and he would always take her outside the living room to talk. I was not comfortable with this, but I refused to ask questions to not be seen as too sensitive and distrusting of him.

One day, the lady refused to follow him and started shouting, asking to be paid today. That was when I realised that a material he gave me during courtship as my Valentine's Day gift, which he said he bought in the market, was collected from this lady on credit and was supposed to have been paid for almost seven months ago. Gradually, different people continued to show up for their money, and I realised that all the things he provided for the engagements were on credit. Each day came with its surprises; things went on unfolding very fast that made me realise I have been scammed into marriage, even though the wedding expenses were almost carried out by my family. My elder brother bought the cow, his wife paid for the cake, my elder sister paid for the event centre. They did all these not because we are so wealthy but because I am the last born baby of the house.

Moreover, our dad died the year before, and it was only my wedding he did not attend. So, they did everything to please me. All my husband did was to bring the bride price and buy other customary things expected of him.

During our pre-wedding class in Church, my husband said he is an accountant and stated his salary, but when cleaning the house after the wedding, I saw his payslip that he is a clerk and the salary is not up to one-third of what he told us he earned. Upon that, he took a loan from a micro-finance bank two years before we met, which he was still paying. He did not tell me all these before we got married. When I asked him what did he do with this loan? After much stress, he said he wanted to travel out, but it did not work out.

I swallowed all these pains, forgave his mistakes and decided to put them behind me. I discussed his employment situation with my pastor, an influential man who could help him get a better job in a better place. So, I told my husband the pastor wanted to see him with his CV and credentials. Providing this became a war. Every day saw my husband giving different excuses. Eventually, he said he left his documents in his mother's house. Without telling him, I went there. His mama said nothing was kept in her house. I was pissed off and went back home, spoiling for a fight. When I confronted him, he then confessed that he was not a graduate, but a Secondary School certificate holder. I was mad! This is someone that is always carrying the Bible and behaving like a saint. He even filled in our wedding forms that he is a graduate. I started playing back everything and realised that 90% of all he told me about himself, which influenced me to fall in love with him, were lies!

He is fake, insincere, a fraud that deceived me into marriage. He could not pay rent, feeding was a problem. He could not do anything. The work he had was a contract job. Not long after the wedding, something happened, and I noticed he was not going again. Bitterness had set in on me, and I refused to ask him anything. It was from his friends I heard that he had lost his job. Neither did he care to tell me. Our relationship had been strained since the certificate matter became clear to me. I had to fall back on my family and friends for help.

Fast forward to today, ten years after he has worked in almost eight places, but they all lasted for a few months and sometimes he stays months at home before getting another. In that period of unemployment, he does not see the necessity of doing something to bring in money. Now that he has a new job outside the state, with a salary of about N50, 000, he hardly sends us money for maintenance. All the little trade I do, I have eaten both the profit and capital. Now, I take goods from people and pay them after selling. I also worked in two different private schools as admin staff, but I had to leave when it turned out to be slavery.

The fact remains that whether I have income or not, my husband leaves everything for me to do. Even when I tell him I have no money with me, and there is no food at home, he sends no money. Now, the children are going to bed on empty stomachs. The hardship I did not see in my parent's house, I have seen it in marriage. Right now, we are just housemates. I see him as someone out to frustrate me. Sometimes, we stay months without sex. Every feeling I have for him is dead. I am the one the landlord asks for rent. I pay the school fees; in fact, I do almost everything. This is the man who was acting like a born again Christian to marry me!

My pastor is aware of everything. He spoke to him and he said he is looking for a job. Before you get the job, will you not do something to take care of your family and assuage the burden on your wife? This marriage is like a bone in my neck! I am tired. I need to escape. I need help. I am just 36 years. I am too young to face this burden!

Counsel:

I sympathise with you concerning your matrimonial dilemma. Marriage is to be enjoyed and not endured, but unfortunately, the latter is your experience. Here are my humble suggestions: First, the Bible says, "If anyone does not provide for his relatives, and especially for his

immediate family, he has denied the faith and is worse than an unbeliever" 1 Timothy 5:8.

Your husband's attitude towards you and the children is a denial of his faith in Christ Jesus. This man does not deserve your love and empathy. I recommend that through the support of family and friends that, you relocate. Look for an apartment you can afford and a school for the children that do not pressure you. For it is better to be a single parent than to continually live with a man that "is worse than an infidel."

On the other hand, you can continue to endure all the emotional abuse, hoping and praying that he will change someday. In any case, the choice is yours. However, for the sake of readers of this book, I want to add that you are part of your predicament. You allowed yourself to be fooled and deceived because you were not sensitive enough to decipher some truths about your

husband when you were courting. Out of desperation, many ladies are too insensitive during courtship. They focus on trivialities and pay less attention to realities. Truth is the most constant thing in this life. A liar always need to cover lies with lies, so there must be a time liars would slipped from what they told you before, but unfortunately, most ladies are too insensitive to know.

UNPROFITABLE RELATIONSHIP: 35

IT IS UNWISE TO ALLOW FACEBOOK CAUSE PROBLEMS IN YOUR HOME

There was a lady on my friends' list on Facebook who lived close to my residence. We do greet when we see on the street. I knew her husband, a Muslim who always wears Jalamia, that long caftan, with fundamentalist beard to match. The lady was also close to my wife, I see them chat in the vicinity. This lady would also post funny things on her wall, comment on my post, we joked a lot online. Suddenly, all these stopped. I stopped seeing her online. I began to wonder what went wrong. One day, we met in a shop, and I asked her what

had happened. She told me she would use her friend's phone to send me her issues with her husband. Below is the (edited) message she sent to my inbox.

"I am more educated than him. He is a school certificate holder while I am a university graduate. I know the benefits of networking more than he does, and I am cautious on Facebook. I present myself as a married woman, using my name and my husband's name.

Recently, a guy I had known, my first boyfriend and my first love, sent me a friend request. Though I was surprised to see him, all the same, I accepted it. In my few chats with him, I told him I am happily married and should please limit his interactions with me. There is no day he would not send me a message which most times I did not respond to. I thought of blocking him at a stage because he was beginning to be romantic. God knows all that was between us was in the past, and I have no feelings for him again. I do not greet him or comment on his wall. I do not even go to his wall.

Five days after we met online, he sent me some birthday greetings, wrote a kind of poem as he did those days and posted it on my wall. He even used my picture as his profile picture. When I saw this, I just laughed and deleted it immediately. I sent a message to his inbox to thank him, but he shouldn't have posted it on my wall, knowing that my husband is also on Facebook, and such acts are morally wrong for married people. I also frowned at using my picture as his DP and told him to remove it immediately. He found a way to laugh over it, saying all sorts of rubbish about how I celebrated my birthday with him those days. I did not respond to such things.

Four days later, in the morning, my husband called me. It sounded as if something had happened.

Pointing his phone at me, he bellowed... "Who is this?" He mentioned his name. Immediately, I knew he had seen it. I got the phone, starred at it and feigned ignorance.

"Who? I do not know him o.' I shouted... "You do not know him, and he used your picture as his profile picture?

"My picture? I got the phone again, the idiot had not removed my picture. I could not deny it again. I knelt before him. I was lost as to what to say. How will he believe me that I am not double-dealing with him? I began to cry as he began to shout, calling me all sorts of names and saying that our marriage was over.

I do not just know what to say. I left him and went to Big mummy, his elder sister, a very educated woman who works in a ministry in Alausa Lagos. I explained everything to her, showed her all my discussions with the guy on Facebook messenger. She saw the guy's wall, got his number and called him. I do not know what they discussed. But she looked satisfied and told me to wipe my tears.

She put me in her car and followed me home, my husband had packed my entire luggage and put them on the street, and I heard he had gone to Ibadan, I am sure to see my parents and his. We both come from there. Big mummy immediately put me in her car, and off we went to Ibadan. There were calls upon calls from our parents on our way. I was just weeping. Big mummy responded to all the calls. She told them not to worry, I was not cheating, and she could swear with the Holy Quran that I was not. That kept my family and his at peace. My husband switched off his phone. He was unreachable.

We went straight to my father's house, where we met him. Big mummy, ten years his senior, spoke and explained all that happened and told him he acted in error. He should have waited. My mother said she knows her daughter, and she was disappointed by my husband, who levelled these accusations. But she knelt for him to please forgive me if he feels hurt.

My mother, a secondary school teacher, collected my phone and smashed it on the floor. She even took a pestle to pound it to pieces. She took the sim card, mangled it with her teeth, and told me never to come on Facebook again. This happened in February. Today is November. I do not have a phone, talk less of being on Facebook or WhatsApp, and my husband is happy I am incommunicado. See my life! All because I am married!

Counsel:

The story above is the marital issue of a Muslim couple; nevertheless, this may as well be experienced in a Christian union. There is nothing extraordinary about her husband's reaction (or action). He felt cheated and betrayed. His trust is broken

despite all evidence not being the actual reality of things. Sincerely speaking, the young man is hurt, and things like this take time to heal.

My advice to the wife, and any Christian wife in a similar situation, is do not allow your experience to break you emotionally since you are not guilty and your conscience is clear before God and man. Be strong and continually be that loving and good wife around your husband. In a matter of time, you will win his trust and love again, and your home will be peaceful and blissful.

UNPROFITABLE RELATIONSHIP: 36

WRECKING YOUR MARRIAGE OVER AN OLD FLAME

In just one week, three people discussed the pains they are encountering over their wives' membership of (their) old students associations.

I was working on a discussion I had with one of the guys when another called on a Saturday morning to share with me his squabbles with his wife on the same issue. Please read my discussion with the last guy, and let's see if it is wise or not for wives to attend such meetings. Do not forget to tell me if your wife attends one. I also want you, women, to speak to husbands on how to handle such matters. So many homes are in quandaries over this issue right now.

HIM: Good morning Bola, the story you shared this morning on the woman having issues with her mother-in-law is similar to my story. When my wife started attending her old students' meetings, she started searching for her old boyfriend on Facebook, etc. I got to know this when I stumbled on her phone and went through her chats. Just as you advised the woman to do with her husband in the last narrative you published, I opened a line of communication with my wife and she became angry. She started talking all sorts of nonsense to me. I was overwhelmed; I lost my cool and gave her some slaps. The next day being Sunday, she went to the Church alone but later came back to apologise to me that it was the devil and that she was sorry about hurting my feelings. Can I still trust my wife?

BOLA: I am the president of my old students' association, Timi Agbale Grammar School, Ede, and some female old students, now wives of some men, attend our meetings. I guess it is a matter of maturity between the members. A woman who knows where she is coming from would not participate in meetings to mess up with old flames. Men who fear God and have self-respect will not attend such meetings to wreck the homes of married women. In my association, we are all matured, and there is no such rubbish, or would I say, such news has not come to my notice. That is how it should be. Let me add that wives must seek the consent of their husbands to attend such meetings and, if possible, they should come together. It could be selfish for men to stop their wives from associating with their old mates, especially female friends.

As the president of my association, some of our female old students told me their husbands do not support their attendance. I knew why. I found myself speaking to some of these husbands that we are mature people, and I am not presiding over a lawless and immoral organisation. Those who believed me allowed their wives to come. So many did not but actively converse with me on happenings in the association and the school –

different strokes for different folks. I have seen the negative sides of the old students association, how it breaks homes. Some men and women, old flames, practically lose control when they see themselves again.

In the early 1990s, as a journalist in the Daily Times, I reported in *Lagos Weekend* the story a lady told me about finding the man who deflowered her and treated her well when she was young, and how the relationship started again. Her husband later found out, and the home broke. Her relationship with the old flame also did not last six months. Such relationships do not last. Never! Women should know this. *Ija lon gbehin ale.* Illicit relationship always ends in a feud. Tell me your story: how did she get involved in the association and get absorbed on the Internet?

HIM: I got married to her two years after we met in a Church where I was the Choirmaster. I was 29, and she was 23. We were blessed with our first child not long after the wedding, and things were moving very well for us. I left my business and joined a company where I rose to become a manager. I bought her an SUV and set her up in an industry that thrived well.

While we were dating, she told me she had a boyfriend while in secondary school and that they were not dating anymore before she gave her life to Christ two years before we met. I later discovered that my wife started searching for her former lover on the internet. I asked her, and she was sober. After some time, she finally saw some of his old relatives on Facebook, and they started chatting. One day, I rechecked her phone and saw a message she sent to her friend about meeting her first love somewhere. I was devastated. Again, I cautioned her, and we reconciled. The lover boy got married two years before us. My wife is very gullible with the opposite sex. She would say she likes to meet with people. I discovered that all her female friends are not married and are not Christians, and these are the type of people she enjoys hanging out with.

Recently, I lost my job, and I sold some of our belongings to set up a new business, but I was duped. I had a setback that made it difficult for me to be financially adequate at home, and my wife began to pick up the responsibilities, meeting the demands at home. She is a seamstress. I am setting up a new promising business in a few months so that at least I will be financially independent. One of her wayward friends called her to join their old school association. She immediately jumped at the idea. She got a new phone to boost her image. When I discovered the change in her attitude, I rechecked her phone and found the guy's name in the list of the members. They held their first meeting in a club somewhere in Lagos, and I remember my wife left the house dressed to kill that day. My wife! Mother of my four lovely children!

BOLA: Did she tell you before going to the meeting?

HIM: She told me. I started seeing her private chats with the guy. I was disappointed. She got back home after their meeting. I decided to ask her again about the guy, and she started talking nonsense. I lost my cool and dealt her some slaps, and I think those slaps woke her up. I have the guy's number, and I want to call him. Right now, she is keeping her phone close to herself.

BOLA: Before a woman would start looking for her ex, something must be happening in the home? What have you done to her?

HIM: I have my faults but not cheating on her. She told me that love alone is not enough in marriage, that money must be available 95 per cent. I have told her not to mention the old school association if she still wants to keep her home. That is my story for now. It is hazardous to marry a beautiful woman, my brother. Our lovemaking is no longer romantic...

BOLA: Do those friends come to your house, or do they go to her shop/office? If she is not responding to you okay, have you discussed the issue with her people or do you care to discuss it with them?

HIM: The friends do not come to our home, they meet her in her shop. She argues that I have not caught her red-handed, that I have no case.
BOLA: The questions are these:
1. Should married women keep the company of single girls?

2. Should married women attend old students' association meetings where they could be exposed to temptations of old flames?

Counsel:

There is nothing wrong with married women keeping company with their single friends. But everything is wrong when a born again married woman keeps company with unbelieving married women and/or single friends. She will be led astray in a matter of time. 2 Corinthians 6:14-15. Also, there is nothing wrong with married women attending old students' association

meetings. If it is not bad for married men to attend, why should it be classified as wrong for married women? Attending old students' meetings is not the only avenue to face sexual temptation(s). Our workplace or church centres could be avenues to be tempted sexually. The subject here is discipline and maturity. If you are not disciplined, you will fall to any sexual advances irrespective of the avenue. However, a married woman can still keep company with her unmarried, separated, divorced or otherwise friends. She can be a tool God would use for their salvation, but friendship must be defined. There must be limits.

UNPROFITABLE RELATIONSHIP: 37

MARRIAGE MATTER: FAITH VERSUS COMMONSENSE

I am a 27 years old man, a young Christian and a member of one of the Nigerian Pentecostal churches. I come from a Muslim background but became a Christian when my mum died. I am from a polygamous home. My father is still a Muslim. The challenges my sisters and I encountered from the other wives of my dad drove us to Christ. And thank God we got results.

I am about to get married in December. I know all her family members. One day, at a beer parlour, someone who knows the family told me some unsavoury news about them, and I later found out that it was true. When I asked her, she confessed and said they did not know what is wrong with their family, and that is why she joined the Mountain of fire.

They are six in her family, four ladies and two men. She is the last born. All her three elder sisters have issues: the first lady is now 13 years in marriage, no issue. The second sister is nine, no issue. The third had a child six years ago but turned out to be an *abuke,* hunchback. Since then, no issue. They kept the child in their village. That is not all, the firstborn, a man, behaves as if he is mentally ill; he can slap anybody anytime. The first day I got to their house, before he knew I was the fiancé to her sister, he almost wrestled me to the floor.

We have been dating for three years. She looks so responsible, prayerful and God-fearing. Most weekends she spends in my place, but I suspect the peculiarity of her family history would not stop her from active sex with me. All my sisters said it is either she is pregnant before we get married to be sure she is fertile, or I let her go. I do not want to get married and start having fertility issues. I want to be careful. I love her very well, but I am afraid. Should I insist on pregnancy before marriage or simply let her go? Deacon Bola, if I am your blood brother, how will you advise me?

Counsel:

I thank the Lord for your life that you attend church services, but I must be sincere with you, you are either not born again or not true to the Christian ethics. Your visit to the beer parlour, soliciting for sex and permitting your fiancée to spend the weekends at your place regularly are indications that your salvation is questionable. And if your salvation is in doubt, then I doubt that you have the faith to weather any storm that may arise in your marital life.

You both need to be sincere with your life and stand in Christ Jesus. You cannot

continue in sin and expect grace to abound, God forbid! Repent.

Thereafter, if you both believe you are meant for each other in Christ, put your faith and absolute trust in the Lord. He will break every yoke (curse) in the family line of your intending partner and bless your union.

UNPROFITABLE RELATIONSHIP: 38 HORRIBLE THINGS I WENT THROUGH WHEN I LOST MY JOB

I am at a crossroads on what to do concerning my wife, or should I say the mother of my two children. I got married to her in 1998 when I was working with an insurance company, and life was good. I occupied a three-bedroom flat, and I had two cars. Believe me, I did all my best to make her and the children comfortable. She is a civil servant.

Six years ago, the insurance company downsized, and I was retrenched. I had gotten a loan to build my house, change my car and do other stuff. All this ate up what I got as gratuity and that was the beginning of my experience for four years.

When her attitude towards me began to change

gradually, I tried to call her attention to it. My wife went to join her old students' association, which I had objected to earlier. You need to see her dressing to Church. She cooks what she likes, without the usual 'Daddy, what are we eating today'? She leaves the house and returns anytime she likes without explanations or apologies. I tried to open communication with her, but it was rebuffed. I began to notice that she might be happy that I lost my job.

The last four years have been a period of losing control of my home. Four years of pains, anguish, slavery and loss of face. That was the same period my wife was promoted in her office, given a car allowance, and she began to live big. At first, I thought it was all a joke until my wife brought in her younger sisters. These were the people who dealt with me on her behalf.

When I could not pay the children's school fees again, hell was let loose on me. She would say it is my responsibility. Of course, she would pay, but after drawing so much heat. I told her to raise some cash so we could finish the house we were building and move in, so we could stop paying rent. My wife said the place I was building was far, and she would prefer we remain where we were as tenants. Please bear in mind that she showed the place to me and we went to buy the land to build.

I stopped getting cooperation from her. She would do things without telling me. Sex at home became when she wanted. Her sisters, two of them, packed in without telling me. When she got the car loan, I asked if we needed another car, when we have two cars already. She said she was tired of driving a Camry. She wanted an SUV because all her mates were driving one. It was like a joke to me. My wife on her own went for the SUV and brought it home. The day she brought home the Lexus jeep, they had a party in the house, called all neighbours and stylishly made it clear to them that she bought it with her own money.

So, because I could not pay the rent again, her

sisters took over everything. They would play music till when they liked. They became the cooks and served me food like a dog. I often look at the meat they gave themselves and what was served to me. Often, when I find two *ponmo* (the skin of cow) in my stew, they would be eating chicken. Uncle Bola, it was like watching a horror film. I could be in the bedroom when the food was served. Nobody would come to tell me. Until I ask and one of them would shout back that *"your food dey table o, or make I go carry loudspeaker shout."* My wife would pretend not to hear such insults. These ladies would not greet me as it is customary for them to do. If we met at the door, they were ready to force themselves in, rather than step aside for me to move on. I must be over 12 years their senior!

They became a kind of threat to my children. One day, one of them slapped my daughter, and I got angry. When I wanted to react, the two of them pounced on me verbally. They told me my story. That was the day I went mad. I pulled my belt and ... My wife's sisters called the police on me. My wife was indoors, pretending to be asleep until the police came. Thank God that my friends rose to my defence. I would have spent the weekend in a police cell for beating two women.

After these experiences, I decided to move out of the house. Our Rev. Father, who had severally intervened, got fed up. One day, he asked me what could I have done to make my wife change so suddenly. It was like the devil entered into her. My wife would chat on *Facebook* or *Whatsapp* till eternity and stopped sleeping on the marital bed. There were times I wanted to physical enforce decency in the house, but when you do not have money... I finally moved out of the house when my blood pressure read 200/140.

My parents raised money for me to rent a room somewhere. Since I got to this new room, my wife did not bother to look for me, but I had my peace because I could buy whatever I needed. Not long after, I had a lady friend, a widow, who warmed my bed. In all of this, I drew close to God. I never kept quiet. My Rev. Father and I kept praying. He told me it was a test of faith, and I would come back stronger.

March last year, I got a job again at the same insurance company. They came to call me at home. God restored me. My captivity was over. It was not only a job, I also got a printing contract worth multi-million naira through a lady. By August, I was back in good form, and I was ready to pick up the pieces of my life. I want to take custody of my children and dissolve the marriage if possible.

The Rev. Father said he is against divorce and I should return to my house and take charge, as it was before losing my job. My parents also said I should return to the home or finish up the building we abandoned and, if my wife still needs the marriage, should be ready to come there. As good as that is, I do not think I need this woman again. I left home over a year ago, she never looked for me. Only on Sundays would my children see me in Church and give them what I have. My wife behaved like a champion in the Church. I was constantly tormented.

I do not know how the news of my change got to her. Five months ago, she came with her family, father, mother, and other relatives to beg. Families I never saw in four years! In my presence, they were abusing her for allowing her sisters to run her home. The SUV she bought had an accident and was a write-off. She has not even finished settling the loan. Uncle Bola, I went to hell and back. I do not want this woman again.

I am not receiving the cooperation of my Rev. Father and my parents for a divorce. It is my life. God delivered me when I moved out of the home and the sight of this woman. By December, my building was ready. I repaired and sold the two cars I packed in the boys' quarter. I added money and bought a new SUV. I am sure the SUV I drove to Church gave me off.

Now, the widow I am dating: Is it proper to ditch her? She kept me busy when I was lonely. I did not promise her anything, but she is good to me. She is also a civil servant in Abuja, 39, Christian, widowed. A top shot at ..., she kept my company, warmed my bed, put money in my pocket, bought food and cooked when I was down. It was through her I got the contract.

She arranged some petty contracts for me while my ordeal lasted, with which I kept going. To her, my heart goes. For a whole year, she stood by me. Is it fair to ditch her? I mean, the mother of my two children has no right or claim on me and my return to life. They are coming back because she now has an issue, and I am back on my feet. Uncle Bola, I am not ready to go back to Egypt. Throughout December, she was coming with her family to plead! Where do I go from here?

Counsel:

I bless the Lord for how things turned out for you career-wise and financially. But truth be told, the relationship between you

and your widow friend is adultery and is unjustifiable before God. There is no denying the role she played in your rising financially, but this is not enough reason to marry her, especially when you are still legally married. The Bible says, "God hates divorce," Malachi2:16.

Sincerely, your wife failed when you most needed her support. So, sensibly speaking, she does not deserve you. But you see, we Christians do not live according to the dictates of our common-sense but by the law of faith and the Spirit of life which is the word of God.

If your wife is honestly sorry for her misconduct, I appeal to you according to the word of God to forgive her and together rebuild your home, Luke 17:3-4.

However, I feel your wife is not sorry yet. Judging from the events of this marriage, the woman does not truly love you. There is

no genuine love in this marriage, so I think it would be disastrous for you to give her another chance. This kind of woman can kill you to get what she wants. You need to face reality and be sure of what you are doing with your life. Did God join you together in the first instance? Are you sure your union was in line with the will of God?

UNPROFITABLE RELATIONSHIP: 39

CAN I EVER TRUST MY MOTHER-IN-LAW AGAIN?

I got married three years ago. My husband's father, who is late, was well known in Nigeria when he was alive. However, like some men without scruples, the father got his housemaid pregnant. The pregnancy became my husband and the maid, my mother-in-law. My husband was unemployed when I got pregnant, but later, he got a job as a contract staff in a bank while I remained unemployed.

I became a member of their Church by marriage, though I am not comfortable attending the same church with his mother. But there is nothing I could do since my husband is largely tied to the aprons of his mother. All through the months of the lockdown in the wake of the spread of the Corona Virus, my husband moved all of us to their family home to stay with his family.

One day, around 6 pm, a Church member was driving by and saw us, my husband, his younger sister, their mum and I, seated outside. The Papa should be in his 60s, and he is very influential in Lagos. It was during the Corona Virus lockdown, and the streets were dry. Immediately he saw us, he parked his car and approached us with a big smile, asking about our welfare generally. Seeing me, he apologised for not attending our wedding and jokingly promised to make it up to me someday. He then asked where I was working, and my husband said I was unemployed. The papa ruefully said he knew how difficult it could be for young couples in times like this when everywhere was in lockdown, adding that all his children are graduates and working abroad with his wife. He said he has a friend in a top position in one of the oil companies, and he would speak to him right away.

There and then, Papa picked up his phone to make a call. As his phone rang and he raised his hands to his ear, my husband's mother stopped him and said if it is an oil company, they should give it to my husband and I can remain unemployed, adding that my husband is just a contract staff in a bank. I was shocked. Papa could not repeat a thing; he just fiddled with his phone for a while and said the network was bad. He bade us farewell and left. My mother-in-law now shouted at my husband to run after Papa to follow through. Since then, my husband has refused to feed me back, and I pretended not to care.

That night I wept badly and called my mum on the phone. She has not said anything till now. But Uncle Bola, why must I experience this from a woman I call mother, that I can remain unemployed and my husband, who already has one, should change? Uncle Bola, I have been a sad woman since then. But I do not know what to do.

Counsel:

Mothers will be mothers, and your mother-in-law is not different. She is only looking out for her son. Most mothers-in-law in her shoe will do likewise, so do not blame her. What is essential is the love, understanding and concord in your relationship with your husband. Let us assume your husband gets the job, your love, agreement and understanding will push you through, and you both will be beneficiaries of it. So, I appeal to you to move on. Better days are ahead of you.

UNPROFITABLE RELATIONSHIP: 40

WHERE DID I GO WRONG HELPING A FRIEND'S WIFE?

There is a friend I met in the church a few years ago. Our friendship grew, and we almost became brothers until I gave my life to Christ, and I stopped doing things we did together: quaffing beer, talking about and chasing women, serenading the nights, going to pubs, etc.

Since I accepted Christ as my Lord and Saviour, I tried to stop him by showing him the foolishness in our lifestyles. He has not changed, and the possibility is not in sight, judging from how he carries on. This makes our friendship drawn apart. We hardly see like before now. We only call and say 'hi, hi'.

I know him so well. He has issues with many of his clients because of his inability to control himself and his desires. If you give him money to take from here to there, something will happen to it. His wife has complained about him to even our pastor and I on several occasions. He hardly pays his children's fees. The wife picks most of the bills. Every evening he is at our drinking joint.

Something happened last week, which is likely to tear us apart finally. It has to do with his wife, who put to bed their third child recently. She runs a shop from where she manages herself and the children. She calls me once in a while to report or ask for favours which I do, even without telling my friend. The woman sees me as his closest friend. Whenever she puts to bed, if I give my friend some money like one hundred thousand naira, all he would give his wife could be less than twenty thousand naira. The balance would go on his binge. Last week, I transferred N150, 000 to the wife's account and then texted him that I sent his wife some money. His response was, why did I not give him the money. I want to snatch his wife, that is why I am tempting her with cash! I thought he was just joking. I just laughed it off.

I was shocked when I saw him in my house the following morning to make some noise that I have no right to give his wife money if my intention is genuine, I am a wife snatcher. That was when I knew he was not joking. My Landlord heard our noise and came out. When he listened to the story, he blamed me that anybody would say I am tempting the woman. Me? Tempt a woman with three children? When has assisting a woman with a useless husband translated into tempting her? I called his wife to tell her what her husband did, she began to weep, begging me to please consider her and not him.

Was I wrong to have sent her money directly, knowing the husband? I mean, I even sent him a text to inform him. How has this become tempting another man's wife? I want to call the woman to please send back my money. Should I? I feel so hurt and regret everything.

Counsel:

A just cause is sometimes persecuted and not appreciated. Your action is indeed noble, considering the situation. According to you, this is not the first time you are assisting the wife; the only difference, in this case, is that you went further to inform the husband, your friend. I see no reason for you to regret your action. Your friend is only a noisemaker; deep down in his heart, he knows the truth; he is not just willing to admit his foolishness.

Move on, my brother. If the opportunity presents itself again for you to help the wife

and children, please do as long as your conscience is clear.

UNPROFITABLE RELATIONSHIP: 41

MY FAMILY IS AGAINST MY FIANCEE

I am 27 years old university graduate. Since I completed my National Youth Service three years ago, I have not been lucky with employment so I started doing some businesses. The businesses support me well such that I could afford to rent and pay for my accommodation and bought a Honda car early this year. My late Dad is from Ogbomoso, my Mum Kwara.

My problem is with my family and the girl I hope to marry. She is Ijebu and a single mother of one. She is beautiful, light in complexion like a half-caste. You can hardly know she is a mother if you were not told. She had the baby boy for a man from her town. If no one tells you she is *after one*, (has a love child), you will not know. She is 18 months older than me.

The day my mum got to know that she is from Ijebu and has a love-child, she decided not to accept her. When this lady came to say hello to her, after greetings and pleasantries, my mum told her point-blank that *Oloun a pese oko rere fun e o*. (God will provide another husband for you). I am sure she understood what my mother meant, and she left quietly. I got angry with my mum that why should she speak to her like that. She responded that I am inexperienced and would not watch me walk into a trap.

My elder sister, fifteen years older, told me that the Ijebu people have a culture whereby a woman with a love-child for an Ijebu man will forever be relating with the family of the man, adding that any time the man's family has a function, she would go there to participate in respect of her love-child.

Another thing I noticed is that all her sisters have children for men they did not marry, except one who is the wife of an Anglican pastor in Lagos. Their mother was also a divorcee but now remarried to someone. The mother, popularly called Alhaja, is neither a Christian nor Muslim. For her, anything goes.

My trouble is that my sisters and mum will not let me take control of my life. They feel I am a small boy. I am a graduate, for God's sake, almost 30 years of age. I am not troubled by these primordial sentiments of one town against the other. I see people as individuals. A whole town cannot be bad. We talk about unity in Nigeria, but here we are drawing on sentiments to truncate my desires.

However, something tells me to be careful. Like my mum would say, I am still a child and have not seen the world as they have. One of my sisters told me that a child cannot see even on a treetop what an elder sees while sitting on the chair. What is the limit of independence? What is the limit of choice? How far can a son go on his own, disobeying the wishes of his family?

Also, I have raised the issue of marrying a single mother with my friends. It is like many of them are not disposed to it. Even women amongst them said they would not allow their sons to marry such women, no matter what. Uncle Bola, what are the challenges involved in marrying a single mother? This babe is still beautiful. I am so confused, Uncle Bola.

In all, I believe I can cope with her. How can I free myself from my family or advise me to let her go? What are the challenges involved in marrying an after-one Ijebu lady? I love her. Pretty. Slender. Lepa. Mulatto. You will not know she is after one. Uncle B, please advise me as your son on this ethnic suspicion and profiling, are they true? Will you allow your son to marry an Ijebu girl?

Counsel:

Marriage is a pretty good thing but, at the same time, very sensitive. Everyone around you is at liberty to advise you on who or who not to marry, but it is still your prerogative to marry who you feel connected to. There is a saying that experience is the best teacher. Your mother, siblings and friends are only expressing their experiences and the traditions of the land. And to an extent, they are the best teacher, John 16:13. When it comes to marriage, you can bank on the leading of the Holy Spirit.

I want to encourage you not to base your decision to marry this lady on the ephemeral qualities like she is beautiful, does not look her age, etc. Beauty is deceitful, Proverbs 31:30, but your willingness to marry her must be borne out of convictions in your heart that she is the one ordained by God for you.

Note, she will not be the first or last to give birth out of wedlock nor will she be the last to spring forth from the Ijebu tribe. The decision is in your court.

However, our people should please do away with judging people based on where they come from. Let us see ourselves as individuals. There are no bad people, no bad towns, no bad countries, no bad nations. There can only be bad individuals.

UNPROFITABLE RELATIONSHIP: 42 MENSES AND SPIRITUAL CLEANLINESS

This case is about my wife and her dirty habits when menstruating. This is not the first or fifth time she would not know her menses is coming, and we would wake up in the morning, and menses would be all over the bed. This has caused problems between us so many times. I always tell her that in my church (I attend a white garment and she attends Pentecostal), and this I believe firmly, menses is a spiritual taboo. It can destroy your prayers. In my Church, women are not barred but are advised to stay away from church or the altar when menstruating. It is an unclean thing. Even you women hate it, how much more we men.

When I raised this, she would say, I hate to see menses, but I can dip my penis inside where the menses comes from. There are times she would say, can I not clean it. I hate to hear this, and it has caused problems between us so many times.

Now, I want to separate our bedroom, let her stay in her room and me in mine. I just found one of the reasons why some men, Christian and Muslims, choose to have a separate bedroom with their wives. I have criticised the habit, but now, I want to follow suit. She reported me to my parents, alleging that I have ulterior motives for separating the bedroom. I am a clearing agent. She is a teacher in primary school.

Now, I want to ask: Is my decision to separate our bedrooms wrong? Do things like this not violate spirituality? What is the Christian understanding of this issue?

VBC.

Counsel:

Menstruation in itself is not dirty nor is it a spiritual taboo. It is what makes a woman, an indication that she can be pregnant. Your wife's menstrual circle has nothing to do with hindrance to your prayer life, but your mannerism in handling this issue can be.

"In the same way, you husbands must give honour to your wives, treat her with understanding as you live together. She may be weaker than you are, but she is your equal partner in God's gift of new life. If you do not treat her as you should, your prayers will not be heard." 1Peter 3:7 NLT

Whether you as the husband have a sperm discharge, or your wife's menses stains the bed, that does not in any way defile your spirituality or your matrimonial bed,

Hebrews 13:4. Your wife is your wife and she, just like you, has her weaknesses. You must learn to tolerate her and, in the spirit of love, admonish her to overcome them. Finally, if your child scratches the body of your car, will you condemn him/her and restrict him/her from entering it ever again? Therefore, separating rooms can never be the solution, but a peaceful resolution will.

UNPROFITABLE RELATIONSHIP: 43

THIS IS AN OLD STORY ...

BUT HOW DO YOU CONSOLE HER?

One blustery Thursday noon, a lady called me. She is a friend I met on social media, and we have stayed as friends ever since. She got in touch with me the first time when her husband decided to emigrate abroad because he was tired of Nigeria. He earns a pittance for a salary, and the children are still young. He felt emigrating would do him good. His wife, a civil servant.

She was sceptical that her marriage would remain if he emigrated. According to her, even when her husband was here, she could not trust him with women even though she has not found him out once. She did not support his relocation, but her husband's elder sister and brother in England advised it and were ready to support him financially. The plan was that he would first go, and she and the children would join him later.

When the lady contacted me, I simply told her she could not stop a man who has made up his mind, especially when he has the support of his family and he feels nothing good can happen to him in Nigeria. Let him go. Support him with prayers. If he is your true husband, he will stay with you. But the fact is once a home is divided, husband abroad and wife in Nigeria, especially for an indefinite period, the chances of sincerity to one another and survival of the marriage is slim, except both parties fear God.

I know that he left early this year, and he was staying with friends. Each time I run into her online, I ask if he is communicating. She would say he calls but has not been sending money; instead, he asks her to send him money, and she has been trying. However, she got a rude shock someday when her husband blocked her on Facebook, she has no access to his account again. He only calls late in the night, and when she raised the issue of Facebook, he would brush the topic aside.

I told her to forget the Facebook matter; his phone could have issues, and she should not expect money from him now because no one picks dollar on the street of America. He needs to find his feet first. The last time I spoke with her was five months ago. This week, I saw her message online that I should call her quickly. I did. She was weeping profusely. What could have happened?

Last Saturday, she and the children spent the weekend with her husband's mother, as they do once in a while since he travelled. She was cleaning the mother's room when she saw an envelope under her bed. She picked it up, intending to put it on the table. The contents felt like pictures. Curiosity made her bring them out of the envelope, and the bubble burst! They were wedding pictures of her husband

and a black lady. She said she froze. Her husband's elder sister and brother were at the wedding. She saw them in the pictures. A note containing a Yoruba female's name and some biblical and Koran verses were in the envelope.

She said the first thing that hit her was to go on Facebook to search that name. She did. She found the lady. On her wall were the same wedding pictures posted on February 6th! Her husband had travelled on January 26th, meaning the relationship must have been on even before he travelled and was known to his family. The lady tagged a man's name. She clicked on the tag, it was her husband with a new name on Facebook.

According to her, she has not confronted the family nor discussed the issue with her husband. All she does now is pity party and weep. But how do you console such a woman? Such pains!

Counsel

This is very sad, and unfortunately, this may likely be the end of your marriage to this man. I, for one, do not encourage long-distance courtship, talk less of long-distance marriage. As earlier said, it takes the fear of God and discipline for such relationships to work.

My dear sister, I feel your pain, but honestly speaking, no amount of weeping or confrontation with his family will bring this man back. Encourage yourself; be strong, and look out for yourself and the children. I trust the Lord God to give you grace and the fortitude to move on in life.

UNPROFITABLE RELATIONSHIP: 44

I DO NOT KNOW WHAT TO SAY ABOUT THIS

I have seen this experience dramatised on our home videos, especially the Yoruba home videos. However, I do not buy that solution.

A friend of mine got married about six years ago, and there has been no issue till now. Last year, he came to me that his mother brought another lady for him to marry as a second wife, adding that immediately she conceives and perhaps put to bed, it will supernaturally pave the way for the first wife to also conceive. According to him, Yoruba people say *ori omo ni npe omo waye,* meaning a new child born in such circumstance always calls to life more of his mates.

I suspect the arrangement was not known to the first wife, whom I know as gentle, cultured, and a believer; neither did my friend see the implication of what he was being led into: polygamy. I also doubt if the new lady knew she would cause sorrows for another woman because of a delay that was not her making and only God could resolve.

I told my friend not to assent to his mother's request because that solution is not from Jesus. Moreover, there is no guarantee that the new lady would conceive and the delay is not the making of his wife. I added that I would never attend the second wedding, would not honour the woman, and I do not want to see her. I am loyal to the wife at home. On that note, he left. I believe I have acted as a good friend and as a Christian.

Early this year, he called me and broke the news that he was forced to marry the new lady brought from the village in October last year, and she is already pregnant. I responded that no one forced him; he loved the idea and went for it. I warned him that what he did was not a Christian solution.

He came up with arguments like he was already 39, at what age would he train children and other sentiments like I do not know how it feels to be childless. That day, I was not ready to drag the matter. It was useless since he had fallen for it.

On a Sunday before the lockdown, as my wife and I were set for church service, his call came and guess what? He said his first wife is pregnant. I congratulated him and asked to speak with the first wife. Her frustration at the prospect of a second wife was unmistakable in her discussion; though she was happy she is pregnant. As a Christian, she insisted God gave her the child, and it bears no link to any second wife. She is sad because her husband did not act like the Christian she thought he is. She is so disappointed and sad. I encouraged her in the Lord and told her to keep a clean heart and bear no grudge against anybody.

During service that Sunday, I was so distracted by the news. Is picking the second wife a solution to issues like this? How does it happen that once a second wife is pregnant, the delayed first wife often get pregnant also? That is not what the Bible tells me. There is no such example in the Holy Book. Are those pregnancies from God? Is this not a trap of polygamy by the devil? No doubt, I am happy for my friend, but I am confused about that 'solution' because I know it is not of Jesus.

A man once responded to this scenario by citing the Abrahamic experience, saying Hagar's pregnancy led to the birth of Isaac. Never! I disagree. Hagar or no Hagar, Ishmael or no Ishmael, the promise of God to Abraham that he would have a son, despite his age, would come to pass. The birth of Isaac is not predicated on the coming of Ishmael. Do you agree with me?

So, why do issues like this happen? Is this of God? Women, if you experience this delay, would you fall for this solution?

Counsel:

Your knowledge of the Scripture on this matter is quite impressive, and I agree with you on your opinions. He who calls himself a Christian, a child of God and falls for deceit like this is worse than an infidel. Isaac and Rebecca waited for twenty years before the birth of Esau and Jacob. Zachariah and Elizabeth were well advanced in their ages before the birth of John the Baptist. There is no amount of excuse that can lower the standard of God concerning the delay in childbirth in marriage. In the Christian faith, there is no room for a second wife; how much more using it as a yardstick for the first wife to conceive.

UNPROFITABLE RELATIONSHIP: 45

AT 44, SHOULD I REMARRY OR STAY SINGLE?

I GOT DIVORCED 14 YEARS AGO BECAUSE MY EX WANTED TO CONVERT ME TO ISLAM, AGAINST OUR EARLIER AGREEMENT THAT I WOULD REMAIN A CHRISTIAN IN THE MARRIAGE. NOW, MY PARENTS AND SIBLINGS WANT ME TO REMARRY, BUT I AM AFRAID AS IF IT WILL CRASH AGAIN. NOW, AT 44 YEARS, CAN I REMARRY OR REMAIN A SINGLE PARENT AS A CHRISTIAN?

SHE: I got divorced 14 years ago with a boy and a girl. My parents want me to get married again, but I am afraid it will crash again. I am now 44 years old. Can I still get married, or I should remain like that? We could not settle our marriage issue because he is a Muslim.

BOLA: Hmmm. People who will speak on this would like to know some background information surrounding your divorce. Can I ask you some questions and will you answer me truthfully?

SHE: Yea, I promise you, sir.

BOLA: Why did you marry him, a Muslim, in the first instance? How did you meet? How did he convince you? Did you inform your parents he was a Muslim? What did they say? Let's start from there...

SHE: Hmmmm!!! I do not know what came over me... Even my parents were against him, but I insisted and got pregnant, so because they do not want an abortion, they agreed and took it as fate. He, too, promised that I would be practising my religion without any problem. And it was so initially until after I had two children for him, and everything changed. I met him in one Cooperative house where he was working then. My parents were bitterly against my marrying him.

BOLA: You said after two children, things changed. What happened?

SHE: He became a chronic Muslim! And he started saying I am the one hindering his life to be successful.

BOLA: What is your age difference? What is the level of his education? What was your level of learning when you married him?

SHE: He was 6yrs older than me. I do not think he had a school cert. But I was an OND holder then.

BOLA: What was the attraction for you to marry him?
SHE: I do not know, though he was neat. That's all

BOLA: Money? Was he giving you good money and good sex?

SHE: Sex came after long persuasions. But good money. And I had money then... I earn good where I worked. Aside from salary, I get daily money too.

BOLA: Remember you promised to tell me the whole truth....
SHE: Yes, sex did not come until a very long time. Even when we did our wedding, my mum and I were the brains that covered him.

BOLA: Now, were you married* with the consent of the families? *Was there an Islamic wedding called Nikkai? How did he become a Chronic Muslim?
SHE: Yes... We first did the introduction, then the court engagement and the wedding party followed. I do not know how he became a chronic Muslim. At our wedding, there was nothing like the Islamic wedding called Nikkai.

BOLA: Before the wedding, was there a clear understanding between the two of you that you will not become a Muslim? Did he agree to that?
SHE: Yes, he agreed. But without the consent of his

father. He said I should agree to it in the presence of his father.

BOLA: And you did?

SHE: Yes. He said he would not know what I am doing since he lives in Lagos and we are in Ibadan.

BOLA: Now, is his father instrumental in his conversion to chronic Muslim, as you said? Did the father call you that you must become a Muslim?

SHE: I want to believe that because on different occasions, he visited us and threatened that he would disown him if he did not stop me from going to Church. He threatened him severally, and I would tell the Baba that he shouldn't worry about that. I told him we serve the same God, just that the way we pray to him is different. I later heard from my husband's mother that she and his father got separated because of this religion issue... She said she did not even breastfeed my husband for a year before they took him from her because her parents, too, did not want her to marry a Muslim.

BOLA: Hmmm. Did you make your findings of this family before going ahead with the marriage? Were you a Christian before the wedding? Did you go to Church? Did you have a personal relationship with your

pastor for guidance? Four questions for you, my dear.

SHE: We did not do any findings. My parent only got to know his father on introduction day. Yes, I am a Christian... We are Anglicans.

BOLA: How old were you when you got married to him? And where was your dad in all of this?

SHE: I was 24+

BOLA: You were not a baby! Now, are you ready to be a Muslim or not?

SHE: You say what? It is too late. I can never be a Muslim. What I did not do when I was young and still with him? Never!

BOLA: Good. Is he asking you to come back? Has he come to beg you?

SHE: I said he's married with children...

BOLA: Does he take care of his children from you? Are the children with him or you? What religion are they doing?

SHE: Haaa! Do not even go there? He has not been doing anything about the children. They are with me. I have been taking them to Church since we were together. They are both Christians. They even changed their names to Christian names. Mariam to Mary. Mubarak to Emmanuel. Emmanuel had his name from birth, I do give birth at a Mission house of an Anglican Church, and he was born on their Emmanuel day, so the Rev gave him that name. I am angry with myself over my mistake. It hurts. Hurts! I was a novice.

***BOLA**: Was he your first love?*
SHE: No. He was the second person.

BOLA: Honestly, when I hear stories like this, it pains me. I hate women falling into errors like this...
SHE: Mine was a pathetic story. No one with my kind of issue in my family. Now on marriage. I am in a dilemma. I am 44 years in May 2020. My mum and siblings have been begging me day and night. My dad was long gone before it happened.

BOLA: Do you want to have more children? If you are married now, and the man said he wants children, can you make new babies at your age or just want a husband for companionship's sake?
SHE: Do you think it is wise to have children my age? My last born will be 18 by August.

BOLA: The decision is yours. If the man you find says he wants, can you?

SHE: I do not have any problem health-wise. But medically, it is not suitable for me? So, I am thinking of marriage for companionship.

BOLA: What do you do professionally? No man wants to marry an idle woman...
SHE: I am a civil servant. Though a middle cadre.

BOLA: The man would like to know if you are married to him, are the children coming to live with the two of you?
SHE: My children are grown up. One is in a higher institution, and the other will be admitted this year by God's grace.

BOLA: Ok Now... The road is clear. I ask the Lord whom we serve to please intervene in your matter. Let the right man locate you. Every pain in your life is cancelled. Your mistakes are forgiven. You will be happy again. In Jesus name, I pray.
SHE: Amen Amen Amen in Jesus name.

Counsel:

My sister, it is up to you to decide whether to remarry or remain a single parent. Do not allow the pressure of persuasion of your parents or any group of persons to mislead you into another relationship. You are not too old to remarry. There are much older women out there, either newlywed or having marriage plans. Either way, if you choose to remarry, make sure you are marrying a man who is born-again, matured and disciplined this time. Someone who will marry you for whom you are and accept your children as well. And if you decide to remain single, please stay away from adultery so as not to sin and cause troubles in other women's homes. Live godly.

UNPROFITABLE RELATIONSHIP: 46

ARE WE NOT DESTROYING MARRIAGE THINKING WE ARE SAVING LIVES?

The Yoruba people have an aphorism: *Obun r'iku oko ti oran mo*, meaning, the habitually dirty woman will find a ready excuse for dirtiness in the mourning period her husband's death.

The same analogy goes for Tinuke, whose life's pattern, attitudes, past expectations would not allow her to find a husband. She is well known as a termagant, brash, unruly with her tongue, careless. She is running into her 30s now. Her response to getting married is, 'Marriage is out for me. I will not allow any man to abuse me or kill me with a knife.'

I have seen so many social media stories on violence in marriage, leading to different views and advice. Everybody has become a marriage counsellor, advising people on abusive marriages, saying marriage is not a must; there is no marriage in heaven; Paul, Jesus, etc., did not marry, all manner of cheap talks.

Many of the people writing these are not enjoying their marriages or people who are out of it. Their prodigal expectations and rampant immorality hinder them from building their homes. In their game of justifying their status as single mothers/fathers, baby mamas, etc., they have started demonising the marriage institution. It is wrong. *Obinrin s'owa nu, oni oun r'ile oko gbe!*

Encouraging people to get out of marriage at the slightest matrimonial challenge is not right. Only when cases of serial abuse and potential dangers are established. Marriage is subject to its challenges. Two different humans from diverse backgrounds to live as one must be fraught with challenges. That is why marriage is an experience of continuous forgiveness.

Recently, a lady ran to her mother, claiming her husband slapped her. The mum told me she followed her to pack her things immediately. I asked the mum, 'did you ask the husband what happened? Before some husbands resort to slaps, do you know the verbal slaps they have received from their wives? If the husband is your son, what would you do?'

I stepped into the matter and found out that the guy, quiet and calm but unemployed, had suffered several bruises on his ego from the razor tongue of his wife. There is nothing this girl cannot say. Nothing! Let me quickly add this: ladies do not marry a man who is not employed. Let the man settle employment first before deciding on marriage.

The time is now for parents to train their children going into the marriage market on how to manage emotions and temper. Let us cease from pushing half-baked wards into marriages, only to come back and say marriage is evil, they kill themselves with knives. Every marriage has its challenges, but marriage is not evil. Despite the difficulties in marriages, many people are enjoying it. Marriage is work; work it out.

Counsel:
Marriage is indeed work, and everyone should work it. It is not sufficient for a man to resort to slaps at his wife's slight provocation, just as it is not right for women to nag till they push their husbands into physical reactions. Wives should know the difference between communication and nagging and the limits of what their husbands could take. Wives should understand that most weak men will not speak or nag, but they often respond with their fists when they are pushed to the wall. The world would not see how the man's ego has been battered but would see their response on the woman. This is why many disagreements in most marriages have resulted in

deaths.

When women are naging, men should take a walk and allow their wives to quieten down. They can return home later to open a line of communication all over again. Men should remember to be the man at all times. That home bears your name. Honour your name.

UNPROFITABLE RELATIONSHIP: 47

CAN YOUR FATHER NOT REMARRY IN PEACE?

In December 2014, a 49 years old man lost his wife in a motor accident around Lokoja. The woman left behind three daughters and two boys, all grown-up. 2018, the Church felt the man had stayed alone enough, and fearing he could fall into temptations, the leaders called him to get a wife so he could continue his life. They cited the examples of Church leaders who remarried three, four, five years after their wives passed on.

As if that was what he was waiting for, he told the leaders that he would not face his children, especially the daughters, because he knew how attached they were to their mother. Suppose the church could call and speak to them. The Church did. The first three daughters, married and well established in Abuja, and the boys, still in the universities, came.

The Church told them they would not like their father, much under 60, to fall into temptation that could ruin his image, standing in Church and record in heaven. The church has therefore proposed to him to get married again, according to the Bible. That was where the problem started!

While the two boys saw reason and supported the move, the three elderly daughters said no way! If it were their mum, they were a hundred per cent sure she would never remarry. Their father would remain a widower till he dies. The daughters stormed out of the meeting, almost abusing the pastor, leaving the boys behind.

They went home to show their Papa hell. Papa told them it was not his idea, however, the Church has an excellent idea to assist him to live long and be away from different women winking at him. The daughters insisted their father would not bring another woman home to sleep on their mother's bed. Which mother? How unreasonable can some women be!

Weeks later, the pastor texted the daughters to please think of their father, still under 60, needing assistance to cook, take care of himself, even feel good sexually. The daughters said they would get him a cook and cleaners, but warming bed with another wife, no other woman would live in the house their mother struggled to build with their Papa. They called their Papa a traitor to his face.

Anyway, late last year, Papa's family, his younger brothers, the daughters' husbands, one of them a senator, including the parents of his late wife, called the daughters and insisted their father must pick his life again. They should not compare a man's life, a widower, with that of a woman. Then a bait for them: they were told to find the wife for their dad. That did the magic. It placated them very well.

Meanwhile, in the mind of the church leaders is a widow in the church, a 49 years old medical doctor with all her children abroad. The widow, too, was ready. She has been going to Papa's house to cook for him, but no one knows what happens after cooking o. People do not see them talk in church but trust choir members, some of them said they have seen Papa and Dr a few times in ShopRite. But now, the Papa is slipping through Dr's fingers.

Last year, the daughters brought the replacement. A Hausa lady, Customs officer, also a widow with five young children. Papa refused. The Church said no. Papa's family, including his late wife's family, disagreed. The Hausa lady from Adamawa has never lived in Lagos. Knows nothing about Yoruba culture. She wants to move in with her young children. It was a no-no for them all.

December, the Church, the daughters' husbands and families went ahead to solemnise the union of Papa and the doctor. The daughters refused to attend the wedding. Now, they are telling whoever cares to listen that they suspect the doctor killed their mother with juju because she was not on good terms with their mother when she was alive. How come she is the one replacing their mum? She killed their mum.

Also, they insist Papa should divide the properties into two, they want to take possession of what belongs to their mother. They fear the new wife would take over what belongs to their mum after killing their Papa. That is the stalemate now!

UNPROFITABLE RELATIONSHIP: 48

TO WHICH OF THE CHURCHES CAN I PAY MY TITHE?

Thank you, Uncle Bola, for your articles that have been shaping my life and thoughts. I like to discuss with you something that is eating me up. I don't mind if you post it, just take off my name. You know I am a Christian, and I believe you know I am a tither since Baby, your wife, and I were in the Anglican church. Just like her, marriage also took me to a Pentecostal church and outside Lagos.

In this Pentecostal church, the pastor knows his people, those he goes to their homes with his prayer team to pray for. I have approached him several times to come to my office to pray for me. He would ask me what am dealing in. I told him. He said OK.

To date, he has not come. But I am aware he visits a woman who has a big shop not too far from my area. When I told my husband, he said I should take my eyes off any pastor, I should be dealing with God directly.

Up till 2017, business was dull for me. So I went to inform my vicar in the Anglican in Lagos, a venerable. This man will drive down here to pray with me every month. There is no week he will not call me to pray with me.

Miraculously, something happened in November 2017. I got a contract, a big one that my tithe was seven digits. In February 2018 again, God did another one. Late February again, God showed up in the most significant way of my life when I sold a property to a company. It was a big one, and I want to pay the entire tithes now.

I told my husband that I would take it to the church of my vicar. That is the man who prayed for me. He gives me Holy Communion. He anoints me. He prays on my business. He believes in me. That was the man who showed me pastoral care. But my husband is saying I should bring the tithe to his Church. I feel this is unfair to my vicar. I feel I should give my tithe to where I get blessed.

Now that my money has come, this pentecostal pastor of my husband will start patronising me. Uncle Bola, where does one pay his tithe? Is it not where you get blessed? After all, it is the same house of God. There is no denomination in heaven.

COUNSEL

First of all, let me correct that language many people use for tithe. You do not pay tithe, you give it. The word 'pay' shows a kind of transaction between you and God. A tithe is a thing to be given willingly and joyfully, not a payment. Payment is always by force. So, kindly use the word 'give' when

it comes to tithing. Now, concerning who or which Church to give your tithe: you give your tithe to where you are being spiritually fed. Besides the fact that your pastor did not come to your shop on your request, are you spiritually fed by the Word in that same such? If yes, then you give it there. You have been in that Church with your husband for how many years? You can give love or sacrificial offering to your vicar. Tithes, offerings and whatever financial investments are not meant for either of these men of God. It is for the furtherance of the work of God. Giving is a seed sown for your good. Also, Madam, please erase the mindset of '... now that my money has come, this Pentecostal pastor will start patronising me...'. It shows you are not in that church but just attending for your husband's sake. (... that pastor, ... my Vicar). If we decide to treat everyone the way they treat(ed) us,

where will our place(s) be as Christians? Bitterness should be dealt with, and forgiveness should be applied towards the pastor for not visiting you, else you will not get the rewards for your giving in the church. Matthew 5:23.Your Vicar prayed for and with you, but he didn't answer the prayers. God did! Do not allow this tithe issue to start a war between you and your husband. Obey him!

UNPROFITABLE RELATIONSHIP: 49

WHAT CAN I DO TO THESE UNCLES?

Pastor, I graduated and served about ten years ago and married two years later. After the wedding, my wife's father, whom I called Daddy, a man who was so good to us gave us two vehicles, a Tokunbo Lexus jeep and a Camry popularly called tiny light.

Daddy did not tell anybody that he gave us the vehicles, so my friends and family thought I bought them. Before the wedding, Daddy gave me money to rent a three-bedroom apartment and paid for five years. He furnished it again. Every month-end, he would send me cash gifts and bags of foodstuffs. On weekends, I would be in his house in the Lekki area of Lagos, where we would sit and talk politics over bottles of wine. Sometimes, I would drive him to the beach where we would *flenjor*. Going back home, he would always give 20k, 40k. So, I loved being with him. Meanwhile, my monthly salary where I work is 70k.

Two years ago, daddy died, and all the largesse stopped. I came back to depending on the 70k salary. But when the beautiful days lasted, I was open hand to my friends and families. I took care of my mum (my dad died long ago) and uncles, even those who did not remember us when our dad died. I always sent them money like 10k each anytime they called me.

Now, the happy days of daddy have passed, but now and then, three of these uncles would keep asking me for money. I could receive five text messages from each of them in a week, coupled with phone calls upon phone calls. These are men who have their children, uncles who did not even give me *shishi* when I was schooling, now disturbing my life. I did what I could to help, but now I can barely help myself. We have three kids and their school fees to cater for. The vehicles, pay rent, foodstuffs, etc. Their calls call run me crazy now.

Yesterday, my wife told me two of them called her for money. I was so mad. How can they call my wife again! Don't they have their children? When my wife saw my anger, she then said they have been calling her for a long time, and she has been sending to them whatever she had. But now, she is not financially ok, that is why she decided to tell me to explain to them to let her be.

Pastor, how do you do this and not attract enmity from these uncles? Can I block their numbers on the phone? Would that take care of the situation?

COUNSEL

The money you ought to have invested, you were doing Father Christmas all about. I am not saying it is not good to give, but you sow on fertile grounds. These men have

their children, why worry you all the time? Maybe you were posing all over town to be a very rich man, and they thought it was right to get their share. I'm sure that their children must have been investing their own money and must have not had enough to give their parents. But you created a wrong impression that is haunting you now. You better tell them the truth and start spending with wisdom. You need to open up to them that the source of free money has shrunk, but don't bring the issue of your cars, children and family into the matter. Initially, it will be tough, they will start talking all sorts and perhaps vilifying you... but stay on your ground that things are not as rosy as they used to be at your place of work.

UNPROFITABLE RELATIONSHIP: 50

OFTEN, MARRIAGE IS A BLACK MARKET

The choice of a partner and living together legally as husband and wife, called marriage, is often a black market. A partner can hide his character for months just to achieve a goal. The heart of man is deep. No one can search it. You often require the power of God to decipher the heart of man. No wonder the Bible says he who finds a wife (and husband too) finds a good thing and receives favour from God. Seriously, getting a good partner is pure favour! It is not by brilliance and perfect calculation. The scripture cannot be broken.

If, after the close of work, you are eager to go home to the warm embrace of your spouse, please learn how to say 'Lord, I thank You.' Why do I say this? Not many men can do this. So many homes are hurting bad, not just because the spouses are weak or lazy, cannot calculate or plan, foolish or that you are more intelligent than them. For some people, things do not just work.

Many people live in self-effacement not to disappoint their friends and families. I have met so many people on social media whose posts and pictures would make you feel they are living in perfect matrimony but, in reality, are in deep matrimonial bitterness and divorce.

Haven't you seen men and women who call themselves marriage counsellors, relationship experts, whose marriages have either collapsed or at the brink of collapse? I have seen plenty of men of God who join people on their wedding days but their own homes in disarray! This is a case of physician, heal thyself! Will not you thank God for your home?

It is easy to blame people whose marriages have failed. It is easy to become a professor of marriage, organising marriage seminars where you speak with panache and authority on the constitution of happy homes, drawing graphs, quoting facts and figures on relationships. Just thank God that things work for you. The Yoruba people in Nigeria have a saying: It is the farmer whose cocoa seedlings grow into a tree that is praised as a good farmer.

Those who become divorcees today did not plan it so. They also had high hopes, but somehow, the story went awry. I have interviewed with so many divorcees in my career as a journalist. Many of them confessed that they had good hopes when their marriages began, but they did not know when their covenants began to slip through their fingers until they collapsed and each party found it difficult to forgive and reconcile.

In chapter four of Chinua Achebe's famous book, Things Fall Apart, Okonkwo calls a fellow clansman a woman after the clansman contradicts him at a village meeting. The man who has no titles, and is, therefore, an *agbala*, was told that the current meeting was for men only. Okonkwo is quickly chastised by his fellow clansmen and an elder that

"Those whose palm-kernels were cracked for them by a benevolent spirit should not forget to be humble." Okonkwo must apologise to the man.

Therefore, if your marriage works, if you can take care of your family, be grateful to God. Be thankful. Be humble also. It is not by your power. You simply received favour from God.

ABOUT THE BOOK

Every day, people file for divorce or walk out of their homes and never return. Why does this happen? Can it be avoided? In most cases, many people who go into relationships and marriage are not prepared for it. A considerable amount of effort goes into wedding, which lasts for just one day, than marriage, which lasts till death do them part. Most parents push their half-baked children into marriages without remembering that poor chaperonage or mentoring would always lead to failure.

I have acted as an online mentor and marriage counsellor to many people who reached me with their matrimonial pains and challenges. Some of the mails sent to me have been presented to men and women of wisdom to give wise counsels in simple terms. I have put these mails together in this book so that youngsters preparing for relationship, courtship, and marriage would be properly mentored before signing the dotted lines.

ABOUT THE AUTHOR

Dr. AdeBola Adewara, journalist, writer and the founding president of Network of African Christian Journalists NACJourn is the editor of E-life, Africa's first internet gospel magazine founded in 2004. The magazine expanded to hard copy in 2017. An infopreneur, webmaster and lecturer in a seminary, he is the author of several books including Become an Internet Evangelist, Discover the Secrets of Mentoring, Marriage: 40 things to know, Message to the Ignorant Church, Diary of an Angry Christian, Truths you won't hear on Sunday service, Unprofitable Relationship: healing for the broken hearts and Conversation on Faith in times like this. Adewara is the host of Mentoring Masterclass, a mentoring programme on Youtube.

Facebook: @Elifemagazine1

Instagram: @boladewara

Twitter: @magazineElife

WhatsApp: wa.me/2348057849480

LinkedIn: @in/e-life/

BOOKS FROM THE SAME AUTHOR

1. So, You Call Yourself a Christian
2. Become an Internet Evangelist
3. Marriage: 40 Things You Must Know
4. Discover the Secrets of Mentoring
5. Unprofitable Relationship
6. Truths You Won't Hear on Sunday Service

www.ingramcontent.com/pod-product-compliance
Lightning Source LLC
LaVergne TN
LVHW041148150826
845673LV00001B/95

* 9 7 8 9 7 8 5 8 8 7 8 8 4 *